D1365072

In the Pink

In the Pink

a memoir

By

Nicholas Garnett

New York, New York

Published by MidTown Publishing Inc.
1001 Avenue of Americas
12th Floor
New York, NY 10018

Publisher's Cataloging-in-Publication data
Names: Garnett, Nicholas, author.
Title: In the Pink: a memoir / by Nicholas Garnett.
Description: New York, NY: Midtown Publishing, 2021.
Identifiers: LCCN:_____ | ISBN:
| 978-1-62677-_____(paperback) | 978-1-62677_____(e-book).
Subjects: LCSH Memoir. | BISAC MEMOIR/
Classification:_____ | DDC _____

Praise for *In the Pink*

Acknowledgments

In the Pink

a memoir

By

Nicholas Garnett

Dedication

"To all the queens — especially you, Mom."

PREFACE

Imagine: the tribal mysticism of Stonehenge, the spectacle of gladiator night at the Coliseum, the debauchery of a sex tour of Bangkok, the constancy and connectedness of a family reunion, the percussive force of a Gene Krupa drum solo, the endurance of twenty-four hours at Le Mans, the explosive joy of VJ Day, the rush (and some of the risk) of cliff diving in Acapulco, and the transformative power of a Lakota Sioux sweat lodge. This was life as a straight, married man in the gay circuit party scene. Or, at least it was. Or, at least, it was to me.

If the metaphors I use to describe the circuit appear to contradict each other, it's for good reason: they reflect the enigmatic nature of the circuit party phenomenon. Since their inception in the eighties, these events have raised millions of dollars for various HIV/AIDS medical research and social support organizations. The circuit has helped to save lives and has provided comfort and dignity to those with AIDS who could not be saved. In a prime example of top-shelf irony, the circuit has also provided the perfect setting for exactly the kind of behavior that spread the disease in the first place.

Though this story recounts actual events, I've changed certain details, including names and occupations for reasons that will become obvious. There was, however, no attempt—and no need—to tweak up the story; anyone who has lived this life can vouch for the fact that the very last thing it needs is embellishment.

1

Baby Steps

"Hey, birthday boy—you lost?"

I turned from the dance floor and there he was—another clone—baby-faced, blond, shirtless, and muscular. He smiled affably, waiting for an answer. I had met him half a dozen times and should have known his name. But I didn't. I bought myself some time. "Lost? As in, am I having an existential crisis? Feeling morally and spiritually bankrupt?"

He raised one eyebrow. "As in, are you so fucked up you lost your wife and friends on the dance floor?"

"Yes."

"Then, let's finish the job." He patted his pocket. "Got a little something-something right here."

I gave up on remembering his name and, instead, considered his offer. The ecstasy had all but worn off; only the slightest tinge remained, soon to be replaced entirely by utter exhaustion.

"Are you implying I need it?" I asked.

He nodded. "Way too serious for the occasion."

I looked out over the packed dance floor. Tomorrow *was* my birthday. What is that thing Rachael always said? "More is more." Besides, this was Saturday night of Pride weekend in New York City, and no one was going anywhere for a long, long while.

I smiled. "Awfully generous of you."

He reached into the front pocket of his jeans and removed the bullet-shaped snuff-snorter attached to a large vial, nearly full of white powder. He gave the bullet a backwards-forwards twist, filling the chamber, and brought it up to my nostril. I inhaled deeply and jerked my head back as it slammed against my sinuses. A chemically tinged sweetness with a hint of vanilla drained down my throat.

"Thanks." I rubbed my nose. "I think."

Now I remembered this guy's name and reputation. Michael Murray—The Ketamine Kid—was notorious for treating his K like a precious commodity, spending hours chopping it up so finely it blasted into your bloodstream like a *blitzkrieg*, sweetening the assault with a little vanilla extract. Michael did some minor-league dealing but was as proud of his handicraft as any artisan, frequently offering up free samples to the unsuspecting.

"Five minutes to blast off," I said.

"It's not for nothing they call it tripping, my man." He administered himself one hit, and then another. Michael leaned forward, palms down, resting his weight on the railing which ran the length of Palladium's mezzanine. He looked on, proud as a lord surveying his land.

The crowd was packed chest-to-chest—a mass of color shifting with the music: red to green to white. After several hours of dancing and layering on drugs like stacks of firewood, everyone was settling in for the long haul—distance runners catching a second wind.

"Hey, Michael," I said, "remember the days when we used to do one hit of X, be home in bed by four a.m., and that was enough?"

Michael clicked his tongue. "Vaguely."

The lights flashed bright.

He tapped my shoulder. "Come on now, don't get nostalgic on me. Go home before dawn? Might as well stay home. Junior doesn't get serious until the sun comes up."

He had a point. The music was potent force, especially when delivered by deejay Junior Vasquez: club icon, protégé of Madonna, and volatile diva in his own right. His specialty was blending songs and beats, wrapping them in nearly sub-sonic bass, and slamming them down on the crowd like a giant, percussive fist. It was the soundtrack to insanity, as powerful as any drug. The music and lights synchronized and began another slow build up, a single snare drum snapping slow eighth notes, increasing tempo, faster and faster, measure after measure, blending to a blur of sound and light, bursting to a new plateau, the base line ripped, the crowd screamed, leapt, reached for the sky. The hair on my arms and the back of my neck rose. Every sense was overloaded, overwhelmed. *There it was.* Everything was brilliant, joyous, connected. The X staged a slight comeback, filling me with warmth and euphoria.

"See what I mean?" Michael yelled. He waved one hand over his head and spun around, dervish-like.

The house lights spun wildly on dozens of crisscrossed aluminum trusses and descended from far above us to rest just above the tallest dancers. Thin strands of green lasers fanned out from each side of the club, tracing broad, slashing vertical arcs. At each corner of the dance floor, muscular go-go boys mounted four floodlit six-foot square black boxes and begin to sway, detached and blasé, as the crowd swirled below them.

Spectacle—no one delivered it like the boys.

"By the way," Michael said. "You'd better sit your ass down somewhere, and soon." He leaned over and planted a kiss on my cheek. "Happy birthday."

I wiped the wet spot with my palm and watched Michael navigate the crowded steps leading down to the dance floor on steady legs, impressive, considering he had done enough K to bring down a wildebeest.

It wouldn't be long before I got nailed like a sharp right cross. I looked around for Rachael, beginning at the center of the dance floor though I knew it was unlikely I'd find her there. That space—downtown—was generally staked out by the largest, highest and horniest boys. Tonight was no exception. Dozens of them had formed a tight, groping conga line, spiraling out from the center like a constellation. Women were not welcomed downtown, not even Rachael.

Then I spotted her. Black patent-leather combat boots, white leather hot pants, and a studded black leather bra top. Her dark mane of hair was arranged the way I liked it best: pulled back, exposing the full lips, dark eyes, brilliant smile. She and Trevor were deep in conversation, oblivious to the two-story bank of speakers pounding out the music just above their heads. Rachael bent forward, convulsed with laughter. Trevor spotted me over Rachael's shoulder, spun her around and, using the cocktail in his left hand, pointed up in my direction. They smiled and waved for me to come down.

That's when the dance floor fractured into angular splinters of color, then reformed into a crystalline carousel, spinning clockwise like a constellation. I closed my eyes and imagined individual particles of ketamine teaming up with the ecstasy, careening through my nervous system like a frenzied Pac Man. My eyes opened to find that Palladium had been filled with automobile-sized fluffy pom-pom balls made of cotton and anthracite. I reached for the mezzanine's railing to steady myself, and, instead, grasped air. Down on the dance floor, bodies were tinged with spectacular auras of orange and cobalt. The music cracked, sending sparks flying from the ceiling in neon shards. Sound faded to a muffled thump, and I was aware of a heartbeat rumbling through my body, down to the dance floor, through the walls up to the ceiling and catapulting straight up to the sky.

I was on the move, an occurrence which vexed me, because I couldn't feel my legs, much less imagine them capable of propulsion. Yet there was no denying the slight rush of air past my face and the flash of smiles and shadows of those I passed. I felt pressure on my arm, glanced down to see a hand clutched to it, just above my elbow. I was being led along by a disembodied hand, which I found oddly comforting.

I arrived before a gold-beaded entranceway. Before me stood an enormous pale man with a shaved head and a tattoo which ran the entire length of his left arm. His face was emblazoned with jagged Maori warrior tattoos. I blinked and they were gone. Something took hold of my wrist and turned it so the big man could inspect. I sensed that this was someone in authority, someone with the ability to make or break my evening—not to mention my arm. I straightened my back and willed myself to focus.

"K or G?" asked the big man, who still had hold of my wrist. The tattoo on his arm, the head of a phoenix rising from the ashes, throbbed to the beat of the music.

I opened my mouth to answer, but from behind me

a voice something like mine said, "It's K. He'll be fine."

I had become a ventriloquist.

The big man said, "Better be. This is a lounge, not a frickin' emergency room."

"No prob-le-mo," I said. "I'm ab-so-lu—" I stuck on the third syllable, partly because of the K, but mostly because I was surprised by the reemergence of my voice from my own throat. I needed to learn how to harness the power of my new-found skill. I tried to give the big man a casual, reassuring thumb up, but there was a good chance the gesture I made looked more like late-stage Parkinson's disease. I wracked my brain for something to say to set him at ease, something casual, but not glib. I laid a Clint Eastwood squint on him, grinned, and pointed both fingers at him as if firing pistols.

He grunted and released my arm. I glided forward and pushed through the beads, which drew themselves across my neck and shoulders like a quilt made of marbles. There I went again, sliding along, a puck on ice, closing in on a padded silver lame banquette coming up hard on my right. Now, the hand was on my left forearm, guiding me like a truck backing into a loading dock. I flopped down and backwards, grateful for the banquette's generous padding. The table-top's polished surface swirled and coiled.

"Stay here," the voice said.

"No prob-le-mo," I said.

The silhouette laughed and disappeared.

Funny thing about K—one second, you're in the spin cycle, the next, you've materialized, as if through the transporter on the *Enterprise*.

The lounge was dim, long and narrow, the walls black and lined with banquettes. At the far end of the room was the deejay booth, the occupant of which was laying it down, softened and sinuous, nothing like Junior's take-no-prisoners assault. The laid-back sound and gentle lighting soften up what was left of my high.

Knots of men and a few women were clustered together at the banquettes, talking, and smoking cigarettes. I looked around to see if anyone had noticed my spastic tightrope act, but no one seemed to be paying the slightest attention.

As if to prove the point, a sinewy, black form appeared from the back of the room. She was all legs and lanky arms as she glided past. The five-inch stiletto heels were a bit much, but they were a look. She wore a short, black leather miniskirt, bustier, and a long, straight, onyx-colored wig. The center of the VIP lounge was her runway, and she was working it hard. Hands on hips, the perfect combination of nonchalance and attitude, she shot past me trailing the scent of sweet perfume.

There was a little hitch in her walk. The heel of her right shoe was loose at the point it attached to the sole. Her Achilles heel. My clever little allusion made me smile. She paused a moment, pivoted her body, and whipped her head around last, just like fashion week in Paris. We locked eyes, just long enough for her to give me a knowing grin. I closed my eyes and watched her image flick and skip forward like a snippet of old film. When I opened them, she was next to me, sliding into the banquette, trapping me against the wall. She smiled, revealing a confusing assortment of teeth.

"Having fun, Papi?" The illusion was shattered. Her voice was Brooklyn, Queens, Puerto Rico with a slight overlay of Telly Savalas.

"Maybe too much," I said. The full force of her

perfume hit me like a whiff from a broken ammonia ampoule.

"Been to this little *soiree* before?"

I sighed, trying to sound blasé. "My second. And you?"

Her laugh rumbled. "Papi, she's a circuit girl through and through."

Why did drag queens refer to themselves in the third person? And why did they always call me Papi?

"This is my sixth," she said.

I tried to look suitably impressed.

"Saw you come in," she said. "You was in quite a state, Papi."

I set her up for the winner. "I'd rather be in your state."

"Which is?"

"*Fabulous.*"

"Mmmm-hhhhhhmmm, honey, what-eva." She waved me off, but I could tell she dug it. She slid a couple of inches closer to me. "What's your name?" Her big, liquid eyes shifted to my chest.

"I thought we decided I'm Papi."

She gave me that husky laugh again. "I'm Bianca," she said, suddenly earnest, like a well-mannered eight-year-old meeting her daddy's boss. She extended her hand, dangling from her narrow wrist.

I touched her hand, and it was all I could do not to jerk mine back. Her fingers were cold and wiry and trembled like the claw of a terrified bird.

"What you doing here alone?" she asked.

"You wouldn't believe me."

"Bianca's heard everything, trust her."

"Trust *me*, Bianca. You haven't."

Her Adam's apple quivered. She placed her hand on my forearm. "Boyfriend trouble?"

I shook my head no.

"Trouble, though."

"I think you're barking up the wrong Papi."

She took my hand in hers and turned it over, leaned forward, and traced one fingernail across my palm. "Ever since I was little, my momma told me I could see things." Her voice was softer now, gentle, and less affected. "She was right."

I shook my head to clear it. Either I was still high as hell or there was something to her. Either way, nothing to lose. I spread my fingers.

My hand hovered inches below her face. Bianca reached across the table and brought over a glass votive, pinched between her slender, dark fingers. She cocked her head. "What's going on, Papi?"

She knew something. Not everything, but something.

"I'm here. Same as you."

She closed her eyes. A shadow skipped across the table. "Not the same. I belong."

I smiled. "Hey, I paid my cover."

She studied my face and squinted, as though peering through fog. My smile vanished. "How'd you get here?"

"Took a cab. You?"

She squeezed my hand. "*Stop playing*. Tell me."

"It's a long story."

"Try making it short."

"How does anybody get anywhere. Baby steps."

"What's that mean?"

"You have to walk before you can run."

She looked me over. "You runnin' now, ain't you?"

She smiled and shook her head. "Talkin' in riddles. Chasing something, like one of them little ducks at the park hustling after their momma."

Neither the notion nor the image sat well with me. I yanked my hand away from Bianca and pressed my palm onto the tabletop. "This is some crazy talk for the VIP room at Palladium."

"Yes it is." She shifted herself away from me. "But there's one thing Bianca knows, Papi."

"What's that?"

"You need to back yourself up and get on out of here."

I grinned. "Something I said?"

She placed her index and middle finger on my forehead. My skin tingled beneath her touch. "Something you didn't say. And those little baby steps? They ain't going to work. It's going to take some big-ass strides to get you where you belong."

I wanted to say something funny but couldn't think of a single thing.

Bianca slid away from me. "You'll excuse me, Papi. The diva is calling." She stood and smoothed the front of her skirt with her hands. "I'm sure you understand."

She did a pirouette and disappeared.

I sat there, rubbing my thighs with my palms. What was that all about? Here I was, sitting smack in the middle of the gayest scene in the world, dressed the part: shirtless, shaved chest, tattoos, leather pants, long hair, drug paraphernalia crammed into every pocket. Why would she think I didn't belong?

"No prob-le-mo?" a voice said. "That the best you could come up with?"

Rachael stood next to me. I should have been

relieved to see her, but I wasn't. "So, I'm not a wordsmith," I said.

"I sent Wes to fetch you. He said you were in no condition to be fetched."

"I'm fine."

All four people in the next banquette had turned around to stare at Rachael and make admiring comments.

"You look rattled," she said.

I was entitled. After all, it wasn't every day I had a mystical connection with a psychic drag queen.

Bianca clomped by and winked. I was relieved she didn't stop to chat. Snide momma-duck references would not have gone over big with Rachael.

"Who's your friend?" she asked.

"Bianca. Odd girl." Bianca paused at the next table, permitting her hand to be kissed with great formality by a shirtless man in skin-tight black patent leather pants.

Rachael pushed the hair out of my eyes. "So, are you feeling better? Everyone's asking where you've been hiding out."

This was one duckling that wasn't going to be rounded up just yet. "I doubt anyone even noticed I'm gone."

Rachael frowned, her strategy derailed. "Okay, I'd like you to come down with me and start enjoying your birthday." She slid onto my lap and put an arm over my shoulder. I wrapped my arms around her, feeling resentful.

"Really," she said, "you don't want to sit up here all alone, do you? Just you and Binaca?"

"It's *Bianca*. Binaca's a breath freshener."

"Come on, Nicky, don't leave me alone on your birthday."

At least she was being honest. Except for the part about using my birthday to guilt me into doing what she wanted.

Rachael slid off and tugged on my hand to follow her. I did, and with her hands holding mine to her shoulders, allowed her to lead me towards the exit. I took small, mincing steps so as not to mash her heels.

"Baby steps," I said.

Rachael turned part way around. "What?"

"Something Bianca and I were discussing."

"That girl is a bad influence."

I nudged her forward, thinking about how it was I got here, and, for the first time, wondering what it might take to get out.

2

Girl Power

Conventional wisdom once held that boys who like boys were the product of outside forces such as the lack of a father figure or the influence of imperious and domineering women. The folks who came up with the theory should have checked with me first. If *that* kind of childhood could make you gay, I'd have sashayed to my junior high school prom clad in a Balenciaga gown, evening gloves, and stiletto heels.

In my world, the women have controlled the chess moves, beginning with my grandmother, the grand master. Anna, a once-beautiful woman with brilliant, emerald-green eyes, had turned the head of many of the men in Athens, including my grandfather, a slender, genteel bank manager, educated in Vienna and fluent in three languages. After World War II, he was hired by the U.S. State Department's Voice of America, a fledgling government agency with the mission to broadcast the truth and the light of democracy to the unenlightened masses of the world.

In 1948, my grandmother and their three children, including my then fourteen-year-old mother, Persephone, boarded a cruise ship for America. They left a life of old-world comfort which included maids, piano lessons, and French tutors, to join my grandfather in Mt. Rainier, Maryland, a non-descript, middle-class neighborhood just outside of Washington, D.C., one commensurate with his government salary. My grandmother, the product of a spoiled upbringing courtesy of a doting father, never forgave her husband for ripping her from her beloved Athens and plunging her into America whose social egalitarianism and nose-to-the-grindstone work ethic she viewed as boorish and beneath her. She spent the rest of her years, all forty of them, getting even by employing an effective combination of utter helplessness and absolute intimidation.

The strategy included self-imposed segregation and isolation, including the inability to communicate in English (except for the most rudimentary words and phrases which she managed to butcher), never working, or learning how to drive a car or write a check. My grandmother was unable to watch a movie in English unless my grandfather was there to provide her with simultaneous translation. In America, the country she badmouthed from morning to night, she kept herself as helpless as a newborn. Within our family, however, my grandmother's rule was absolute, her ruthlessness a match for that of any banana republic dictator.

That's not to say she didn't have her lighter side, like the one portrayed in those old propaganda newsreels showing the merciless strongman on a good day, yucking it up with his underlings, petting a dog, or pinching the cheek of a child. My grandmother could be gregarious and funny, especially in social situations in which she was the center of attention. She was a good storyteller, often recounting her brother's exploits during the war as part of the resistance, the charms of pre-war Athens, or Greek mythology. A repository of folksy old-wives' tales, quirky expressions, superstitions and myths, my grandmother had the ability to deliver a quip with the timing of a stand-up comedienne. She could carry a tune, croon the popular love ballads from her youth, or break into a traditional folk dance around the coffee table. On holidays, or when the mood struck her, she would create authentic and delicious multi-course feasts, complete with heaping platters of lamb, moussaka, pasticcio, spanakopita, trays of baklava, and, my grandfather's favorite, galactobourico, a creamy, phyllo-dough concoction which tastes much better than it sounds.

Then, without provocation, or at least none that could be accurately predicted, she would employ her weapon of choice—a vicious, black rage which she unleashed with unvarying results—the derailment and disruption of any semblance of normal family life. My grandmother's anger was slash-and-burn, a full-frontal assault, during which she would work her way relentlessly through everyone and everything that deserved to be sent to hell. It was a list which included, but was not limited to:

- the Turks
- the Jews
- black people
- Americans (except for Jerry Lewis whose manic physical comedy made her laugh and Kirk Douglas whose rugged, good looks made her swoon—both, oddly enough, Jews)
- any President after John Kennedy (or, for that matter, before)

- my grandfather's side of the family
- the military junta that ruled Greece from 1967-1974
- Henry Kissinger (whose adherence to *realpolitik* lead to U.S. support of the aforementioned)
- The CIA (Ibid)
- Israel (see, *the Jews*)
- American food (she might have had a point here)
- American music
- Come to think of it, just about any person, place, or thing with origins that could not be traced back to Greece.

She'd often punctuate her curses with the Greek gesture of derision, the palm-out swat of the hand, the *muja*, which she enjoyed using on unsuspecting Americans who, thinking she was saying hello, would often wave back to her.

Though my grandmother's hate list was long, it was also peripheral. The hub of her anger was invariably and tightly wound around a family member who was guilty of some slight or lack of deference. Once my grandmother's fury was unleashed, resistance was futile. Challenging her upped the ante, and she was always holding more chips. If my grandmother had been a prize fighter, she'd have had it all—the relentless jab, the ferocious left hook, and the wind to go fifteen rounds. No one could out yell, out curse, or outlast her. Argue with her and she'd bury you in a torrent of profanity and the glare of her demonic eyes which reminded me of the creepy gypsy woman from the *Wolfman* movies. Slap her (as I saw my grandfather do only once after she'd had at him for two days straight), and she'd come at you with her fists or whatever she could get a hold of (in this instance, a bowl of meatballs).

Like a besieged army, all we could do is hunker down and wait her out. In the whole world, there were three things my grandmother loved unwaveringly: Greek composer Mikis Theodorakis, best known for his soundtrack to *Zorba the Greek*; my grandparents' elderly, diminutive, devoted, and submissive black housekeeper Rosa; and her first grandchild, me.

Though my grandfather was the most frequent recipient of my grandmother's wrath, none of her children were spared, especially my mother. Perhaps my mother's beauty reminded my grandmother of the fact that she was no longer beautiful. Perhaps it was the fact that she was the first born and my grandfather's favorite. Whatever the reason, my mother's relationship with her mother was, at its best, one of mutual disdain.

As adolescents, my mother and her siblings had begged my grandfather to do the right thing, by which they meant *leave his wife*. Motivated by some combination of love, guilt, obligation and masochism, my grandfather refused. In response, his children voted with their feet and their identities. Aunt Mary changed her name to Mardi (she thought it hipper) and learned to play the drums. She married the first of five husbands, a gentle-natured saxophone player, and moved to Greenwich Village to live like a bohemian. My uncle

John was drafted into the Army, moved to California, married a Swedish woman, had a daughter, and began chasing women.

My mother, Persephone, whose nickname in Greek, "Phony," had unfortunate connotations in English, changed her name to Yvonne and chose a local escape route in the form of a good-looking, not terribly bright Italian cab driver named George Bono, whom she married, never loved, and who would not become my father.

In August of 1957, my mother and grandmother boarded a cruise ship bound for Greece, a vacation that, given the volatile nature of their relationship, seems preposterously ill-advised. On my dresser, I have a framed copy of a picture taken on that cruise. It shows my mother and grandmother seated next to each other at a long table strewn with post-dinner detritus, including half-filled water glasses, bread plates, and empty bottles of wine. My mother, poised and feline, is turned toward the camera, a cigarette dangling from her manicured fingers, her wrist barely resting on the arm of her chair. Her smile is small and sly. Over her shoulder looms my grandmother, her body thrust awkwardly towards the camera as if she fears being left out of the frame. Her black cat-eye sunglasses obscure her portentous eyes, heavy red lipstick coats her taut lips. She's not smiling.

Following an Atlantic crossing marked by incessant quarrelling, my mother and grandmother arrived in Athens and did their best not to cross paths. That summer, my mother had a brief, torrid affair with a handsome, poor, happy-go-lucky Athenian musician named Illias He impregnated her, but he wouldn't become my father either.

At the end of the summer, my mother arrived back in America pregnant. George Bono may not have been very smart, but he managed to put things together. There was drama, divorce, and scandal. Following my birth, the decision was made that I would live with my grandparents until my mother's life became a suitable one in which to raise a child. For the next four years I lived with a *ya-ya* I called Ma-Ma and was visited by a mother I called Yvonne.

It's possible I represented my grandmother's last chance to made amends for the way she had treated her own children, but there's no doubt I also served as the bludgeon she used to punish and control my mother. Whatever the motivation, my grandmother showered me with attention, treated me as the golden child, gave me anything I wanted, all the while never passing up an opportunity to remind my mother of every single thing she did for me. At my grandparents' insistence, I was enrolled in kindergarten at a private Greek Orthodox school at which I learned to speak and spell in Greek even before I could do so in English. This fluency, combined with my grandmother's insistence that only Greek be spoken in her home, resulted in my ability to communicate with my grandmother far more effectively than any of her children, whose Greek language skills had begun to atrophy as they assimilated themselves into American culture. I was swathed in an all-consuming and oppressive love in which I felt both nurtured and menaced, never forgetting that her adoration would be withdrawn if I ever crossed her. I made it my business never to do so.

My mother's relationship to me became tinged with an element of guilt on her part for conceiving me out of wedlock and for giving me up to my grandmother. As for my relationship with my grandmother, my mother viewed it as a necessary evil, one she was unwilling to challenge or subvert. Instead, she chose, consciously or not, to lash back at my grandmother with the one weapon at her disposal: her choice in men.

When I was four years old, my mother married a funny, wise-cracking, beer drinking aspiring singer and writer, fresh out of the army, who had fled his small Pennsylvania mining town and his strict Seventh Day Adventist upbringing. In the process, he also changed his name—from Carmin to the more show-biz-viable Vance. My grandparents didn't approve of him, but at least my mother was married.

When I was four, I went to live with my mother and Vance in their small one-bedroom apartment on Colorado Avenue in Washington, D.C. My mother was a legal secretary. In between his singing gigs, writing, and waiting for the big break, Vance managed a movie theater; delivered Charles Chips pretzels and potato chips (I preferred the pretzels); drank too much with his buddies; taught me to appreciate jazz, Hemingway, Groucho, and Bogart; loved me like a son and became my father.

By the time I was twelve, my father's drinking had gotten the best of his marriage, and he and my mother divorced. My mother and I settled in Silver Spring, Maryland, a suburb of Washington, D.C., where she dated a series of men—nice enough, but notably lacking in their ability to earn a living.

Now that my mother was single again, my grandparents felt justified about intervening in our lives, presumably on my behalf. Their methods were not subtle. When one of my mother's boyfriends moved in with us, my grandparents showed up at our door. My grandmother burst in, cursing in Greek, slapping, and kicking the guy around the apartment, calling him a bum. The police came. He left.

In response, my mother kicked things up a notch. Actually, it was more than a notch. As far as my grandmother was concerned, it was more like a quantum leap. My mother began to date black men. For a while, my mother kept her latest phase a secret from my grandparents. When she got serious with one of them, however, it was left to me to break the news. I tried the angle that he was light-skinned, possibly a mulatto, thinking that might help soften my grandmother's reaction. It didn't.

Since I was the only one in the family spared my grandmother's rage, I was often dispatched to act as a palliative, or more accurately, a commando dropped behind enemy lines to ascertain her level of combat effectiveness and initiate the terms of the cease fire. I became skilled in the art of acquiescence.

I emerged from adolescence imbued with the attributes of both the spoiled and the abused child: I lacked resilience and initiative yet had a strong sense of entitlement. I was self-conscious, unconfident, easily discouraged, reticent, and immensely fearful of confrontation. I wasn't competitive enough to win, and yet I hated to lose. Though I got decent grades, I drifted, disengaged, though high school and college. I had few close friends. I drank some and did drugs—smoked pot, dropped acid, tried cocaine—but no more than anyone else seemed to be doing at the time. Well, okay, maybe a little more.

When I was seventeen, I lost my virginity to a pretty, blonde, volatile sixteen-year-old named Kathy. Kathy's father had died when she was young, and she had grown up wild and promiscuous. I kept my lack of sexual experience a secret from her, fearing she would reject me. She didn't. We stayed together for three years, had sex frequently and became increasingly careless regarding contraception. One afternoon, I sat in a Planned Parenthood clinic, wracked by shame, as a nurse demonstrated how to slide a condom onto an object I would later come to know as a dildo, while somewhere in the back, Kathy had an abortion. My subsequent relationships with women were infrequent, but serious and long term.

I didn't date, I mated.

My first prolonged exposure to gay men occurred during high school and college, when I worked part-time in the dining hall at the campus of the George Meany Labor Study Center, under the supervision of its flamboyant, mercurial food service director, Billy Dennis. This was the late seventies, with gay culture in its unabashed, pre-AIDS heyday. Mr. Dennis hired only young, cute, straight guys to work in the dining hall and it was there that I and the rest of "his boys," as he referred to us, learned to manage his combination of paternal benevolence, despotism, and explosive tirades.

This was a game I knew how to play. Very quickly, I became one of Billy Dennis's favorites. For my birthday one year, he took me and the other boys to D.C.'s infamous leather bar, the Eagle, which was set deep amidst the ruins of a city which would not recover fully from the ravages of the riots following the assassination of Martin Luther King for another twenty years. Inside the Eagle, we walked around, timid but amazed, stopping to gawk at the counter displaying an assortment of sex paraphernalia whose purpose we could only imagine. Tawdry. But, far from being put off by the scene, I enjoyed all the attention we received from the staff and patrons, shocked and titillated at the sight of a bunch of straight boys corralled in a leather bar.

In the meantime, my mother, disillusioned by her romantic relationships with men who'd brought nothing to the table except their appetites, began to surround herself with the kind of males she could count on. Beginning with her beloved hairdresser and roommate, Larry, these men flocked to her, drawn by her looks, her sense of irony, her penchant for the dramatic, her vulnerability, and her accepting nature. My mother soon presided over a cabal of queens. There was Joe the interior designer, Jean-Claude the secretary, Cary the schoolteacher, Ian the dog groomer, and on and on.

In them, my mother had finally found the qualities she'd always sought in a man: loyalty, humor, devotion, generosity, and a love of Billie Holiday. I can still picture my mother surrounded by them all, watching *The Women* or listening to the soundtrack from *West Side Story*. This was the first time, but not the last, I would witness the affirmation, bordering on exultation, gay men could shower on certain women. My mother, who'd grown up with nothing remotely like unconditional affection, now had all she could handle. I would never see her happier.

Looking back, I can see that I envied her. I was a loner, but not by choice. I graduated from the University of Maryland with a degree in history and political science and no clear idea of what to do with myself. Through an employment agency, I landed a job with a trade association representing the commercial and industrial *insulation* industry, which should be all I need to say about that job. I wandered into a series of progressively higher-paying positions with other non-profits. Eventually, I became Director of Marketing for a housing-related organization, which was run by a hard-drinking, hard-driving tyrant. At staff meetings, he liked to compare the organization to a hockey team, in which only some would make the cut. I didn't.

I ditched it all and turned my hobby, playing drums, into a vocation of sorts. My band, Motif, specialized in weddings and upscale receptions. It was comprised of working professionals for whom the band provided their one creative outlet. The bass player had a PhD in mathematics, the saxophone player was a lobbyist, and the keyboard player was a federal parole officer. What we lacked in musical virtuosity we made up for in the attributes that really matter: showing up on time and the ability to correctly pronounce the names of the wedding party. To make ends meet, I delivered flowers for Rose Express, which was owned by a couple of guys who met at Brown University and came up with the gimmick of having their roses delivered by tuxedo-clad delivery men.

Safe to say that I wasn't exactly at the top of my game. Hell, I didn't even know the name of the game at which I was failing. All I knew was there *had* to be something bigger and better out there, if I could just figure out a way to find it.

Turns out, it found me.

3

Of All the Gin Joints

1991—Washington, D.C.

I stood at the long, stainless steel bar at Perry's, trying to get the attention of the lanky bartender who has spent the last several minutes making me feel invisible. Finally, he stopped chatting up the boozed-up girl at the far end of the bar and ambled over. I had been standing here so long I forgot what I wanted to drink.

"He'll have what I'm having," said a voice from behind me.

I turned. What makes one face interesting and another irresistible? It's something in the eyes, which in her case glimmered like polished mahogany. She had a touch of Ava Gardner. And hey, even a touch of Ava Gardner could stop you in your tracks. Just ask Frank Sinatra, who could have had any woman in the world but took one look at Gardner and started acting like a love-struck teenager.

"Remember me?" she asked.

It was the voice I remembered: low, on the verge of husky. Nothing like the thin whine that could transform the most attractive woman into your bratty niece. Rachael was a vestige from my corporate past, one of the few pleasant ones. I had met her years earlier when I was producing special events and she was director of sales for a large hotel chain. Unlike some of the other hotel reps that came to call on me, there hadn't been any heat between us. But I didn't recall her reminding me of Ava Gardner, either. Last I had heard, she had traded the hotel business for currency exchange.

"You look great," I said. "Have you lost weight or something?"

"I won't even pretend I don't love you for asking."

The bartender cleared his throat. Rachael ordered a round of cocktails for the table, plus a vodka soda for me, and handed the bartender her credit card.

"You don't have to do that," I said.

Rachael ignored me. "Listen, are you hungry? I'm about done here, and I'm starving. We can catch up."

Was I an excuse for her to ditch her workmates? No matter. I needed an escape route every bit as much as she. Maybe more. Besides, what were the odds I was going to stumble across a *better* offer. "Sure thing," I said.

I hung out at the bar, sipped my cocktail, and watched her say her goodbyes. The guys had their ties loosened and their shirt sleeves rolled partway up their forearms in a display of contrived informality. A couple of the girls turned to look at me, then whispered something to each other. Office gossip—I didn't miss that. In fact, there wasn't much I missed about that whole scene. Still, looking around the table at all those young faces, there was something to be said about the sense that the world was expanding. The upward part of upwardly mobile.

We walked the couple of blocks over to Red Sea, where we scored a cozy and private deuce in the bay window overlooking Eighteenth Street. I ordered the sample platter.

"This neighborhood sure has changed," Rachael said.

I followed her gaze out the window onto the busy street: cars and cabs at a standstill, people walking by, chatting and grinning, purposeful. I lived not three blocks away but had often felt like a stranger in my own world. "Thoroughly gentrified. Still a little scary, though."

"How so?" she asked.

"Beware the yuppie scum."

She sighed. "I like the buzz, though. It's young. Makes me feel young."

"That's a pretty jaded attitude for someone your age."

"You want to see jaded, wait a few weeks until I turn thirty."

The waitress came over and set an enormous platter between us.

"Have you ever had Ethiopian?" I scooped up a small mound of spiced lentils with the flat, spongy injera bread. Rachael did the same to the lamb stew. "It can take a little getting used to."

"First time. Most of my eating out is business dinners. We try to save our hands for more practical matters."

"Such as?"

"Backstabbing."

Over the rest of dinner and a couple carafes of wine we joked and parried, mostly about me. I drank in the attention nearly as fast as the pinot grigio.

"So, how do you like your job?" I asked.

"Mostly it's good. Currency trading is so different

than the hotel business, which is full of pretty people who skate by serving the real corporate players."

"Of which you are one."

"Supposedly." Rachael pulled out a cigarette from her purse and pointed it at me. "You mind?"

"Nope."

She lit up, took a long drag, and exhaled through the corner of her mouth. She was all sharp angles—right down to the smoking. No one I knew smoked. Not since my mother, who finally kicked her two-pack-a-day habit, and my grandmother, who used to occasionally lift one of those absurdly expensive Dunhills out of a ridiculous silver case and not inhale.

"So, what are you up to?" she asked. "Still working for non-profits?"

I'd been hoping against hope my work situation wouldn't come up. "No. I've decided to pursue my talent for melting down under stress."

"You got off the hamster wheel? Congrats."

"Thanks. But I have to do all sorts of very unimpressive stuff to get by." I hoped she wouldn't press me for specifics. I wasn't quite ready to put my head on a chopping block and hand her the axe.

She said, "Like I don't? You think I want to hang out with those self-absorbed kids? You're smart. You're attractive. You could do anything you want."

I replied without thinking. "I keep telling myself there has to be more to life. So far, I remain unconvinced."

Rachael dipped her chin. "Sounds like you need a vacation. From yourself."

I looked down at my food.

"Maybe you haven't found the right fit," she said.

"I took one of those tests in a magazine, you know,

the kind that matches your personality type with your career?"

"And?"

"I should be a priest."

"What's stopping you?"

"I don't do well with authority figures."

Rachael laughed. "Okay, Father Nick. Now, to the love life. Seeing anyone?"

"No. The last woman I saw had the outrageous notion that a thirty-two-year-old guy should have some idea of what to do with his life."

"My," she said, "you take self-deprecation to a whole new level." She paused. "So, how is it being single?"

"It has its moments. Unfortunately, many of them include loneliness, boredom, and abstinence."

She shook her head. "I wouldn't want to be out there alone. So, what do you do with yourself? You can skip the obvious."

"The gym, read, movies. Occasionally, I take myself out for a drink. Like tonight. At least until you intervened." I scoop up the last of the potatoes and peas.

"Sorry to butt in." Rachael watched me for a moment. The smoke from her cigarette formed white, wispy curlicues. "Sounds like you need a benefactor."

"Become a kept man?" I shrugged. "Suppose it depends on who's doing the keeping."

"Most of my friends are gay men. You could have your pick of sugar-daddies."

Interesting. Rachael even looked like my mother. They both had those impossibly dark eyes. "The sugar part would work, but not the daddy."

"Really? So many of the men I know are discovering their feminine side. Every time I meet a good-looking man who's not dating, my gaydar starts making a funny beeping noise."

"You should get that looked into."

The waitress passed by. Rachael caught her eye and motioned for the check.

"How's um . . .?"

"David," she said.

"Sorry, I'm terrible with names."

"He's good. The most stable guy I know. Same job, same hobbies. Same David."

Was that admiration or boredom in her voice? I checked her finger for a ring. She had slender fingers, all ringless.

"You guys married?"

"Probably get around to it someday." Either she was avoiding the topic, or it didn't hold her interest. The waitress brought the bill. "Here's something we haven't discussed." She handed her credit card to the waiter, who took it away.

"What's that?"

"Recreational drug use."

"Do you often bring this up with clients?"

"You're not a client anymore."

"Fair enough. What drug, specifically?"

"Cocaine. Specifically."

"First you pick up dinner, and now you offer me cocaine? I thought the eighties were over."

"Gone but not forgotten. I still have a closet full of suits with giant shoulder pads to prove it."

"Sure. Besides, I'd like to finally meet David."

"He's on a business trip."

The evening had just taken a turn. But to where? I slugged down the rest of my wine.

We walked to a nearby parking lot and waited for Rachael's car to be brought out. A minute later, a slate-gray Jaguar XJ6 came up the ramp. I had a thing for British cars, ever since the little Triumph convertible I drove in college. The angle of the ramp gave me a perfect view of the license plate: PNS NV.

"You drive my dream car and name it penis envy?" I asked.

"You get it. You'd be surprised how many people don't." She walked to the passenger side. "You drive."

We headed up Sixteenth Street, the business district giving way to stately brownstones. The conversation turned to small talk. Someone observing us stopped at a red light would note a stylish couple in a stylish car headed uptown following drinks and dinner at some stylish restaurant, no doubt headed to their stylish home. The thought gave rise in me to the overwhelming feeling of impersonating someone, of playing a role in someone else's story, the details of which had yet to be revealed—even to him.

With Rachael directing me, we headed west and crossed Rock Creek Park into Chevy Chase, the high-end side of town. I pulled up in front of a white, two-story bungalow, cut the engine and put the car in park. "Nice digs. How long have you guys lived here?"

"Almost seven years."

I'd never lived anywhere for seven years, not even as a kid—especially not as a kid. We moved a lot. Sometimes there was a reason: to Englewood, New Jersey, so my father could be closer to jobs in New York City; to Miami, where he landed a gig on a cruise ship. Sometimes, it seemed we moved just to move.

We got out of the car and headed up the walkway.

It was a real house, solid looking, not like those tacky mansions they had slapped up in the suburbs. As we reached the walk leading to the front porch, there was muffled barking. I hadn't figured her for a dog person.

"All right, girls." She fumbled with her keys.

I held the screen door open for her as she unlocked the front door. Two snouts wedged between it and the frame, swinging it out towards us. There was a blur of wagging tails, ears, teeth, and dank breath. The dogs, medium-sized lab mixes, burst past us barking, spinning, and panting. The larger, brown one jumped up, planting its paws squarely on my chest.

"They like you," Rachael said.

"It's mutual."

"Right answer. You may enter."

I straightened and tried to brush the dog hair off my pants and sweater.

"Don't bother," she said. "There's plenty more where that came from."

I took a few steps into the living room. To my right was a big stone fireplace and a mantle full of framed photos. The room smelled faintly of wood smoke from the half-burned log lying across the andirons. There was a long, gray, overstuffed sofa against one wall faced by two matching black leather club chairs. I took a few more steps, onto an expensive-looking red-toned Oriental rug. This was the home of grown-ups.

Rachael dropped her purse on the glass-topped coffee table, walked over to a chrome floor lamp and clicked it on. I shoved my hands in my pockets. My confidence was gone, replaced by enormous relief that I hadn't stood outside this front door wearing a tuxedo and holding a box of roses.

"I have to let the dogs out," she said. "Vodka and something?"

"Please."

"Be right back." Rachael disappeared around the corner with the dogs at her heels.

I walked over to the mantle above the fireplace. There were several photos of Rachael and a handsome, but noticeably older man—David I presumed. They stood front of the pyramids, on a beach, and in the mountains. I paused at a silver frame with a photo of Rachael standing alone, wearing a red tank top and shorts. She was as I remembered her, with shorter hair and softer, more rounded features.

Rachael returned, holding a silver tray on which were set two tumblers filled to the brim. She set the tray on the coffee table, lifted both cocktails, walked over to where I was standing, and handed me a drink.

I took a swig, then motioned to the photograph. "Where was this taken?"

"Madrid. About five years ago. The last trip I'll ever take with my parents."

"Why is that?"

"No need to leave the country to get in screaming matches with my mother and father." She paused. "Follow me."

I walked behind her to the sofa and took a seat. From behind a stack of magazines, Rachael slid an ornate silver cigarette box, which she opened revealing a sandwich bag full of cocaine; a small, round, coke-encrusted mirror; a couple of striped straws, the kind from a fast-food joint, cut at an angle; and a rusty razor blade. I watched her scoop some coke onto the mirror using one of the straws. Using the razor blade, she cut it into four fluffy, fat lines.

Rachael handed me the mirror and a straw.

I snorted and pinched my nostrils closed. Rachael did a whole line, half in each nostril, then leaned back into the sofa, the mirror still in her lap.

"That's better," she said.

It certainly was. My fingertips were tingling the way they did when I was either thrilled or terrified. Or, in this case, both.

"I'll be back," she said. She handed me the mirror. "Help yourself."

Rachael started for the stairs, giving me another unobstructed view of her. The dogs padded into the living room, sated and calm. They plopped down on the rug in front of me, panting and wagging their tails. The evening had taken a turn, all right—straight down Nefarious Lane. I looked down at the mirror, the reflection of my face distorted and partially obscured by a dusting of white powder. I put the mirror on the arm of the sofa and did another line.

I felt good. In fact, I felt *very* good.

Rachael came back down the stairs. She wore a pair of short cut-off jeans and a black T-shirt with the sleeves rolled up. She was barefoot. Ms. Corporate Big-wig Rachael had morphed into Daisy-*Dukes-of-Hazzard* Rachael.

"I couldn't stay in those clothes one more minute. And neither should you." She tossed me something. "Here. That sweater looks warm."

I caught a white, ribbed tank top, which smelled of bleach. I stood, yanked my sweater over my head, and tossed it over the arm of the sofa. I took a little longer than I needed to put on the T-shirt. Rachael didn't even pretend not to stare. Finally, she walked over next to the fireplace and opened a built-in cabinet, exposing stereo components. She knelt and started pushing buttons. A disco song I hadn't heard in a long time boomed from the speakers.

"Who's this?" I asked.

"My beloved Sylvester, may he rest in peace."

Rachael spun and twisted in a stylized dance. "When I lived at home, my friend Trevor and I would sneak out to The Pier. They'd play this two, three times a night." Rachael turned a little circle and landed back on the sofa right next to me.

It was now or never. I reached over, put my hand behind her neck and kissed her, not too hard or too long. I let go and observed her reaction. She was motionless, staring at me wide eyed. Her eyes shifted ever so slightly, as though she couldn't decide on which part of my face to focus.

"Whoa," she said.

"Whoa?" I said. "As in *what the hell are you doing*, or whoa, *I didn't expect that*, or whoa, *that felt really good*?"

Rachael slid over, straddling me, her thighs squeezing the sides of my hips. She grabbed my hair, pulled my head back, and kissed me hard. I brought my hands up around her waist and pulled her closer. My hands worked up and down her back, over her breasts, then down to her thighs. She broke away and studied me again. "I don't do this."

"Neither do I," I said.

We were at it again. I tried to lift her shirt, but Rachael found my right hand with her left and squeezed it. She stood, yanking me from the sofa.

We walked hand in hand towards the staircase, not

looking at each other. I didn't know what she was thinking, and I tried not to care, to stay focused on the moment and not worry about the fact that Rachael might as well have been married, that I was high as a kite, that I was very likely in way over my head. The dogs lurched up and followed us to the base of the stairs.

Rachael stopped suddenly. "Wait."

This was it. She had come to her senses and was about to boot my ass out the door.

"Bring the coke."

"Uh, sure." I walked over to the coffee table and gathered everything onto the tray. Rachael and the dogs stood crowded at the base of the stairs. They looked like I felt, which was plenty aroused and just as anxious. The four of us started up the stairs together. The steps groaned, the dogs panted, their nails clattered against the wood. The little family was turning in for the night. Problem was, this wasn't *my* little family.

4

The In Crowd

The next day, I had planned on a bike ride through Rock Creek Park. That and other solo activities would be postponed. For a decade. That morning, a Saturday as I recall, was a spectacular example of mid-October splendor, complete with sparkling sunshine and trees ablaze in hues of ochre and orange. We would spend that entire day inside, lying in bed with Rachael's head in the crook of my arm.

She laid it all out. She loved David, but, at forty-eight, he was close to twenty years older than she, and the difference in age was beginning to show. She had her life before her, while David was ready to settle down and in. More and more, their relationship felt like a friendship. I listened quietly and nodded supportively, the implications of what she was saying creeping through me like indigo ink dripped into water. I'd figured last night for a drunken, coked-out one-night stand between a couple of bored, lonely people looking for something they didn't know they never had. I was wrong about the one-night stand.

For the next ten days, we spent every minute of our free time together. Over long dinners and walks through her neighborhood with the dogs, the bond between us began to set like quick-dry cement. She seemed interested, genuinely interested—in me. She was quick and silly and razor sharp. We could talk about anything. I made her laugh, hard and often, sometimes to the point of tears, her arm on my shoulder to support her as she let out a staccato, breathless hack.

After a few days, I got up the nerve to bring her to my apartment, which, to my relief she found adorable and shockingly neat. We walked hand in hand around my neighborhood, Rachael commenting on its youthful vibe as we ducked in and out of the boutiques, her telling me she hadn't felt so young in years.

I was falling. I began to believe Rachael and I could be together, to imagine myself in her world, and to covet it. This wasn't just a romance. It was the gateway to another life, one defined by possibilities rather than limits.

I had grown up moving from place to place, my family trying to stay half a step ahead of the bill collectors. When Rachael spoke of her future, and then ours, it was as though I had suddenly been given the opportunity to jump out of my sad little novella and into a multi-volume epic.

It was sometime around day seven that Rachael decided. That evening, we sat on the sofa in her book-lined den.

"Think about this, girl," I said, "Think about this hard. You're talking about almost ten years with him. All this life, all this stuff." I motioned around the room. "You're not going to regret leaving it?"

I glanced over at her, slid my hand behind her neck and kneaded it. She leaned back, shot me that beaming smile, pulled my hand from behind her head and kissed my palm. "You're young. You're handsome. You're smart and you're kind. Together, we can do whatever the hell we want. This is our time."

"I'm not exactly the catch of the century. Or the month, for that matter."

She placed two fingers over my lips. "You're just a little lost. You'll find your way. Start believing and watch what happens. Deal?"

"Deal."

She was willing to risk everything. For me. At the time, I thought it was Rachael with everything to lose.

Three days later, David returned from his business trip. Rachael met him at Dulles Airport, intending to wait and break the news to him at home. Instead, she burst into tears and confessed everything, right there inside the terminal. David was shocked, then furious. The next day, he changed all the locks and Rachael moved in with me. She had left it all behind, even the dogs.

What followed were several weeks of emotional whack-a-mole. There were Rachael's mercurial swings in mood, from elation over a new romance to despair over the loss of David and the comfortable life they had constructed, not to mention the realization that the legal agreement she had signed with David when they had purchased their house meant she forfeited all her investment and equity.

That's not to say Rachael and I were reclusive. Rachael wasted no time in forging ahead with her new life and integrating me into it. First off, my rose delivery days were over. Rachael told me I should take my time and figure out what I really wanted to do.

To her friends, however, Rachael's decision to leave David had been as shocking as it was scandalous. Given the circumstances of the breakup, their sympathies were skewed solidly in his direction. It didn't help matters that David was now referring to me as the "disco boy" who'd stolen his woman.

Rachael approached the challenge of having her friends accept me by putting her extensive marketing and public relations experience to work—on me. The movie version of this process would be a montage, beginning with excursions to high-end clothiers, outfitting me with a new wardrobe, picking out things I could never afford, such as tailor-made suits, blazers, shirts that showed off my build, pants that draped just so. Then, it was off to a chichi salon in Georgetown owned by a couple of Rachael's friends, where I was coiffed, manicured, and given my first facial.

Once retooled, I was rolled out to her skeptical public. Phase one involved a series of intimate meals in expensive restaurants where I could meet her inner circle, followed by a succession of appearances at cocktail and dinner parties. I knew that if I wanted Rachael, I would have to sell myself to her friends. Fortunately, I could draw upon my experiences with the entourage my mother cultivated after she and my father split. Rachael's friends displayed the same devotion-verging-on-idolatry to her as my mother's friends had. But there were differences, primarily in status and accomplishment. While my mother's friends scraped by, Rachael's clan represented a thick slice of D.C.'s A-list gay men, including doctors, attorneys, consultants, and business owners. Outwardly, at least, these were confident, secure men, reveling in their success and flaunting it with cool cars, beautiful clothes, and impeccably decorated homes. Over cocktails and cocaine, there was talk of Human Rights Coalition fundraisers, the cost of kitchen renovations, vacations to Tuscany, and second homes in Rehoboth. At first, Rachael took the lead, but it wasn't long until I was beating her to the punch with the funny quip or the well-timed compliment. The reviews came in on me and they were favorable.

As a kid, every time my mother referred to me as the "sensitive" boy, I cringed. Sensitive, I thought, was simply a euphemism for weak. But here were people who acknowledged and appreciated my qualities. I felt as though I'd spent my whole life standing on the wrong side of the velvet rope and had at last gotten the nod from all the doormen.

All, that is, but one. Trevor was short, smart, and supremely confident. Unlike most gay men who were busy at the time shearing, plucking, and waxing themselves smooth as Barbie dolls, Trevor sported a hairy chest and thick, mutton-chop sideburns. The chef and owner of Beck and Call, a popular Dupont Circle restaurant and lounge, he was not only Rachael's oldest friend, but also her first sex partner—though his distinct preference for men was always a poorly-kept secret. When Trevor was sixteen, his wealthy, orthodox Jewish parents discovered his proclivity, kicked him out of the house, and disowned him.

Rachael took Trevor's misfortune as an opportunity to escape her own dysfunctional household, dominated by a raging father who spared his four daughters neither the wrath nor the rod. Rachael and Trevor split the rent on an apartment and lived together for a while until she went away to study fashion design in Miami.

Trevor's resistance to me wasn't overt. But while the rest of Rachael's friends, including Trevor's genteel, tawny-haired boyfriend, Wes, who supplemented his income as an interior designer by dealing drugs, were warm and welcoming, Trevor was cool, polite, and nothing more. Though his rebukes chilled rather than seared, they stung nonetheless. My attempts at humor were received with a patronizing chuckle, and my attempts to engage him, an emotional stiff arm. When I mentioned Trevor's attitude towards me to Rachael, she told me not to take it personally. Trevor, she said, served up sarcasm as readily as the entrees at his restaurant. Give it some time, she assured me. He'd come around.

About a month after we began seeing each other, just a few days before Thanksgiving, Rachael decided that we would take the vacation to Miami she and David had planned. The plane tickets were paid for, the hotel reservations already made. "Why let it all go to waste?" she asked.

Why indeed? Here was a chance for us to be alone, to catch our breath, away from the stress, the scene, and the show.

Or, so I thought.

5

Boy Beach

We stood at the edge of the beach at Ocean Drive at Twelfth Street. For as far as I could see in both directions bright umbrellas lined the pale sand, set under multicolored kites which hovered above, and lifeguard stands hunkered below, sproutingodd, jutting angles. Strung along the length of Ocean Drive was a row of pastel-colored hotels, which gleamed in the shimmering sun. Before me lay South Beach, its star in full ascent, spectacular and surreal, a crazy mash-up of leggy models, muscle boys, hustlers, and hipsters, striding down Ocean Drive past inscrutable old Jewish ladies in their saggy knee-high stockings, sitting on cheap lawn chairs outside their run-down hotels.

We crossed the sand to where two large rainbow flags set on tall poles snapped in the breeze. They were obvious but unnecessary territorial boundary markers. Everyone was very much on display, preening, their bathing suits adjusted just so, their eyes busy scanning and assessing as they sipped their cocktails. Boom boxes belted out bass-heavy four-four beats. Men bounced from group to group, like buff, beautiful frogs on lily pads made of sand. The purposeful flirting reminded me of the college mixers I'd gone to with my frat friends, minus the belching, stale beer and puking in the back seat of my car.

It was as though I had been allowed inside one of those fantastic Fifth Avenue department store displays at Christmas time. I felt out of sorts, but not out of place.

"Welcome to boy beach," Rachael said. "Pay attention to the eyebrows," she added, as we dumped our beach bags on two empty lounge chairs next to a purple and mint colored lifeguard stand. "From the eyes up, most straight guys look like they had a lobotomy. Gay boys' eyebrows flutter like butterfly wings."

We paid the attendant for the lounge chairs, asked him for an umbrella, and got ourselves settled. As soon as we did, I heard someone call out Rachael's name. He was my height and very tan, with dark eyes and a square, heavy jaw, capped by close-cropped, peroxide-white hair. He was wide in the shoulders, thick through the chest, with narrow hips and slender legs. The one attribute I could not help notice was barely contained by his red Speedo. I stood as Rachael introduced him as Hector. He ignored my outstretched hand and, before I could react, kissed me full on the lips. It was matter of fact—confident rather than flirtatious. As Hector and Rachael made small talk, Hector stood with his legs spread, shifting his weight from side to side. I glanced down at the front of my own bathing suit. At least my arms were bigger than his.

"We'll see you later at the Warsaw," Hector said.

"Right," I said, as if I had the slightest idea what he was talking about.

Hector left, picking his way through the lounge chairs, umbrellas, and thumping boom boxes.

"Who is he?" I asked.

"Hector Flores. He heads up St. Barts, the biggest AIDS clinic in New York City. A rock star in that community. He's also known as the cha-cha doctor of

Chelsea."

"And the Warsaw?"

"You'll see."

I flopped face down on the lounge chair and thought about how it would feel to be gay. When I was ten, my friend and I spotted two guys making out against a chain link fence behind a parking lot. When we told my friend's father about the incident, he made us swear never to go near men like that. They were sick, he explained, perverts, which is what we would become if we had anything to do with them, as if perversion was contagious. To the extent I thought of homosexuality at all, I lumped it in with all the other moral maladies grownups warned us about, like shooting heroin and listening to Black Sabbath. I spent my adolescence, the early seventies, clueless about gay culture even as it insinuated its way into the mainstream by way of Bowie and Glam Rock. My friends and I loved a band named Queen fronted by the flamboyant Freddie Mercury and *still* didn't get it.

Now, I did. These guys seemed to have it all. Who would dream of calling them sissies? If anything, they were hyper-masculine, pounding weights, slugging supplements, slamming steroids. No one in their right mind would take on some of the guys hanging out on the beach that day, plenty of whom looked as though they could break me in half with one hand as they sipped their margarita in the other. It seemed that gay culture had come roaring out of the closet and right into society's face, literally. Everyone was kissing on the lips when they met or said goodbye, even in public—making out and holding hands, too—as if to dare somebody to make something of it. Of course, the same behavior that went over in Miami

Beach, San Francisco, or New York City would very likely get one's ass kicked in Macon. But there was no denying that contemporary gay culture had created an attractive, seductive lifestyle.

Just how seductive? To Rachael, who preferred men, but appreciated women, my hard-wired hetero orientation seemed, well—queer. Maybe she had a point. I pictured myself with Hector. No denying, the man was attractive. We embraced. Kissed.

Nothing.

The Greeks, the Romans—they didn't let gender get in the way. What if heterosexuality was just an artificial social construct, imposed by a homophobic power structure?

Feeling oppressed and empowered, I shifted around on the lounge chair. There, not twenty feet away from me standing in knee-deep water, was a bare-breasted blonde. I noticed the gentle arc of her back; the tendrils of a tattoo creeping over the top of her bathing suit bottom; the way her shoulders drew back and tensed; the ripple of her thigh muscles; the rivulets of water dripping down her neck, over her breasts.

Damn.

The Cuntessa

I woke to everything dark and hushed, the whir of traffic blending with the sound of the ocean. Rachael was sound asleep, her head on my chest, a trickle of drool running down from the corner of her mouth.

I glanced at the clock by the bed. "It's ten."

"Ten what?" she mumbled, not opening her eyes.

"P.M. Let's get this party started." I rolled away from her and slid a pillow under her head. Rachael hugged it, turned onto her stomach, and groaned.

"I'm sleepy."

"Sleepy, my ass. You made me promise to get you up. This was your idea, remember?"

"Pour me some sugar."

I walked over to her makeup bag, found the baggie with the cocaine, and cleared a space on the glass-topped bedside table. Using her credit card, I arranged the coke into two fat lines, rolled up the bill, leaned over and snorted one. Rachael tossed off the covers, raised herself up to her elbows, and rubbed her nose with her fist.

"I'm getting in the shower," I said. She looked lovely in the ghostly pale light filtering through the shear curtains. I leaned over and swept the tips of my fingers from her neck, between her breasts, and across her belly. I stood, turned, and headed toward the bathroom.

"Hey," she said. Her voice soft and low. "Come

here."

I knew that tone and what it meant. She sat up on the edge of the bed and motioned me to her. Rachael told me she was well into her twenties before she'd had her first orgasm, and even with me, a partner she claimed to find irresistible, it was hit and miss—mostly miss. Not this time. Our sex was sharp and purposeful. I bore down on her until her body rocked and spasmed, then went slack.

An hour later, we stood in our underwear as I watched Rachael stack outfit combinations across the length of the king-sized bed. "Okay, Lewis and Clark," I said, waiving my hand over the piles of clothes. "We're here for what, three days?"

She regarded the clothes like a chess champion contemplating her next move. "This is Miami. I can't even wear my glasses. Women aren't caught dead going out clubbing with glasses." I followed her into the bathroom where she began to arrange her makeup into neat rows across the top of the toilet. "That studious, hipster look might fly up North, but down here every night is glamour night. By the way," she looked at my reflection in the bathroom mirror. "What are *you* wearing?"

I stepped into the room, put on my white polo shirt, blue jeans, black Reeboks and reappeared.

Rachael stifled a laugh. "Let's rethink your outfit. You want to blend, right?"

"Do I?"

"A straight guy walking into a gay nightclub dressed like that? Might as well hang a sign on you that says 'Eviscerate Me.'"

I didn't feel like changing, but I sure didn't want to be pegged as some dorky yokel. "So, what then?"

Using the lipstick as a pointer, she worked her way

around my body. "Lose the shirt. And those sneakers. The jeans are fine; your ass looks good in them."

I turned and looked at myself in the mirror. "Got to admit, I never really thought that much about my ass."

"Trust me, women and fags, we're obsessed with asses—ours and everyone else's. Wear your black boots and, let's see, the sleeveless black shirt from that place on Washington Avenue. You know. The one that shows off your chest."

The prospect of wearing that ensemble to a gay club made me squirm. "You sure it's not too—too?"

"Too what? Too sexy? Honey, you're beautiful and I want everyone to see how beautiful you are."

"Patronized *and* objectified?"

"Get used to it."

I tightened the laces on my army-style boots, put on the tank top, and walked over to her in the bathroom where she was bent over, blow drying her hair.

"Oh, you look fabulous," she yelled over the whir of the motor. "I could never get David to dress like that. Not that it mattered much in those rinky-dink bars in Rehoboth. Spin around."

I did. "How's my ass?"

Rachael gave me a thumbs up.

"So," I said, "can you enlighten me about what tonight is all about?"

"A circuit party. They started as AIDS fundraisers. Now they're like a Grateful Dead tour for gay men." She clicked off the blow dryer. "Now, help me decide what *I'm* going to wear."

It was fun watching her try on various outfit combinations—fun, that is, until I looked over at the clock. "Do you know it's midnight? Hector told us not to come later than midnight or we'd get stuck in line."

"Five minutes," she said. "Promise."

Twenty minutes and two costume changes later, she was satisfied. So was I. She has selected skin-tight patent leather jeans, matching patent leather combat boots, and a white vinyl halter top. She wore her shoulder-length dark hair pulled back in a tight ponytail. Rachael had the remarkable ability to transform herself from pretty to stunning by accentuating her best features: lips, cheekbones, and her enormous brown eyes. Combined with her even and brilliant white teeth, the result was startling—classic, glamorous beauty. I stood behind her in the bathroom and watched her apply a couple of precisely placed dabs of blush.

"How did you learn to do that?"

"The makeup?" She snapped the compact closed. "I started looking at fashion magazines and trying to copy the models. About the same time I began sneaking out of the house with Trevor to go to gay bars."

"One thing I don't understand," I say. "What does a fifteen-year-old girl get out of going to gay bars?"

"She *gets* out of her fucked up house, the one with the father that hits her all the time, the one with the clueless mother that ignores it all, and she *gets* all the attention any girl could ever want from the most attractive men in the world."

"Attractive men who have no interest in sleeping with you."

"Definitely worth the tradeoff. Unfortunately, there aren't that many straight men like you out there. Not ones who actually like women."

"Since when do straight guys not like women?"

"Most of the straight guys I know wouldn't have

anything to do with women if it weren't for the sex. That's why I gravitate to the fags. No agenda."

Until then, I had never really made the distinction between lusting for and liking women. It had never occurred to me not to respect them. Women may not have always behaved in ways that deserved respect, but they sure commanded it.

Rachael finished with her makeup, turned to me and stood with her palms turned out. "Well?"

I backed out of the bathroom to look her over. "You know, if the whole currency trading thing doesn't pan out, you can always grow a foot taller and fall back on modeling."

She smacked her lips together to smooth the lipstick. "If I was a foot taller, I'd rule the world."

The Warsaw Ballroom was pummeling music, green lasers knifing through gray smoke, air as thick as axle grease, charged energy—manic, primal, and sexual—so strong it hummed through me like voltage. We stood halfway up the staircase to the VIP lounge, surrounded by hundreds of sweaty, shirtless men, a smattering of barely dressed women, and a few striking drag queens.

The vestiges of the deco-era ballroom the Warsaw used to be survived in the fluted marble columns that divided the space and the enormous gilt-rimmed mirrors above the bar. Other than that, there was not much to connect the place with its past. People danced on anything and everything that would support their weight, including shoulder-high black boxes, on top of the bar, across a stage, on massive speakers. It was frenzy, like standing on an outcropping of rocks surrounded by a torrent of white-water rapids.

Hector, who'd just returned from the dance floor, was soaked in sweat. He put his arm around me. "Having fun?"

I motioned to the dance floor. "Not as much as they are?"

"Beats the alternative."

"Which is?"

"Sitting home and wasting away."

I looked around at the crowd, buff and beautiful.

"They don't look sick to me."

Hector gave me a look that told me he knew better. "Get on disability and find a cheap place in South Beach. Keep on partying, until you can't."

My experience with AIDS had been limited to my mother's friends. I remembered her friend Jean-Claude, lying in the hospital, shriveled and wheezing.

Rachael leaned over. "You ready?"

"Ready?" I said, louder than I intended. "For what?"

She looked puzzled. "To go in."

"Where?" I asked. "There's nowhere to go."

"We didn't come her to watch other people have fun."

I had counted on the purple pill Rachael had slipped in my mouth an hour earlier to break the ice. But I felt nothing. Everywhere, men were kissing and groping. From somewhere deep inside, off went a hetero alarm I didn't even know I had, complete with warning buzzers and flashing lights. Hector slipped past me, grasped my hand, I took Rachael's, and our fragile little train threaded its way down the steps and through the crowd, wedged between hot, slick bodies. I was disoriented by the music, the crush of flesh and the flashing lights. Some of these men were huge and some were hairy, and many were both. The stubble on their backs raked against me. What *was* that smell. Antiseptic, like a doctor's office.

"Poppers," Rachael yelled to me over her shoulder.

I hadn't smelled them since college when the girl I was dancing with stuck a bottle under my nose and brought me to my knees. We found some people Hector knew, wide eyed and dripping sweat. When they saw us, they reacted like excited puppies, yelling and jumping up and down. We exchanged hugs. The heat was infernal.

Rachael leaned over and yelled in my ear, "Off with that shirt."

Just behind Rachael, one man licked the sweat off another's chest. I shook my head no. Rachael opened her mouth to say something, but, at that moment, the music faded. Over the PA, a voice blared, "Okay, boys and girls, let's give a big cracked-out Warsaw Ballroom welcome to our favorite messes, The Trailer Park Trio." The crowd whooped. "First up, Miss Bessie." Bessie was skinny and shriveled, dressed like a plantation-era maid with a giant pillow stuffed in the back of her housedress.

"Next, let's hear it for the o-so-hearty Miss Hanna-Burger-Helper." The crowd groaned at the sight of her, crammed into a five-foot frame, her lumpy thighs scraped together through her white pantyhose as she shuffled along in pink, fuzzy slippers.

"And now, making a special appearance, just in from her Double-Wide world tour, let's welcome the incomparable one, The *Cun-tes-sa*," he elongated the name as if announcing the champion of a professional wrestling match. With good reason. The Cuntessa was well over six feet tall, with the shoulders and build of a power lifter. She wore a shiny green evening gown, open-toed sandals, a two-foot-high red beehive hairdo, and a smear of red lipstick. Her putty-colored makeup ran down her massive neck in thick channels of sweat.

Hector leaned over and said, "You're in for a treat. I hired her for my clinic's Christmas party."

I tried to imagine the kind of Christmas party that would feature someone named The Cuntessa. I couldn't. There was a familiar tinkling piano introduction. The Trailer Park Trio grabbed cordless mics off stands and sat, legs crossed, on cheap lawn chairs, the kind with thin plastic straps that carve divots into the back of your legs.

The Cuntessa launched into the first line of Sinatra's "Lady Is a Tramp," followed by Bessie and Hanna. The spotlights tracked from one to the other. Not bad, especially the way they all stayed in character, slouching, chewing gum, rocking their crossed legs.

The trumpet section and drums built to the second verse. The trio stood and gathered close together, center stage. They were swinging hard, shoulder to shoulder, snapping their fingers. I couldn't help wondering what the Rat Pack would have made of these three. The crowd was with them now, clapping to the drummer's backbeat, headed to the slamming big finish. Everyone screamed yelled as the Trio took deep, theatrical bows and then gave everyone the finger.

Lights came down and the low thump of the dance music returned. For the first time since we arrived, I was enjoying myself. I turned to tell Rachael how I felt. Her eyelids had drooped to half-mast, as if she'd just woken up and might drift off again at any moment. Her pupils were dilated, shifting her mahogany eyes to solid ebony.

I touched the side of her face. It was warm and dewy. She grinned, but it was small, crooked, and goofy—not the big splashy smile I was used to. She tugged at the bottom of my shirt. I let her slide it over my head, then tucked the shirt in the waistband of my jeans, just like everyone else. As soon as I did, a large hand attached to a hairy forearm reached over my shoulder. I could easily have pulled away, but I didn't. The hand stroked my chest before vanishing as quickly as it had appeared.

Rachael placed her tiny, warm hands on my stomach. Something was happening, more than Rachael's reassuring smile, more than Sinatra-singing drag queens. Between Rachael's hands, deep inside my belly grew a warm, electric ball, a blend of euphoria and jitters, like the anticipation of sex with an excellent lover. The glow spread through my legs and up to my neck. Sweat ran down my chest and forehead. Despite the heat, an icy wave passed through. I swallowed, grabbed the bottle of water I had stashed in my back pocket, and took a long, slow drink. It spread through me, cleansing and pure. The music was visceral—delicious. I could taste it, savory and succulent. The bass line shuddered up from the floor into my gut and synchronized with my heartbeat. Lights blazed, burst, and shifted with the music. I felt weightless, as if suspended in tepid salt water.

I smiled and caught Rachael's knowing, conspiratorial grin. She was so beautiful, unguarded. Warm, glowing waves passed between us. She rubbed the sides of my waist, kissed me on the lips, and leaned her head on my chest. I dropped my chin to rest it on the top of her head and relaxed, letting the warmth wash over me, feeling her flow into me. Someone leaned their broad, muscular back against mine. We moved together in small, rhythmic, and synchronous circles. Immense, relentless swells of euphoria pulsed through me, flooding my brain, my body.

Everything made sense now, as if I'd been gazing into a shattered mirror which had suddenly been reassembled. The Warsaw Ballroom and everyone in it was throbbing, surging with life, full of heat and music and muscle and sex and smoke and sweat. I was part of it. And now, it was part of me.

A Change is Gonna' Come

My idea of a dance club had been formed in the seventies when I'd briefly dated a girl who ate, slept, and breathed disco. She dragged me out a few times to D.C.'s wannabe-versions of Studio 54, and I tried to fit in. My most vivid memories of that era include swarthy Middle Eastern guys in loud rayon shirts, promising, but never delivering, cocaine to leggy blondes.

Nothing in my past could have properly prepared me for that night at the Warsaw. And nothing in the real world, the one we stepped back into when we returned to D.C., could quite measure up. Of course it couldn't. The circuit was imagined, created, and designed by masters of illusion and theatrics—gay men living under the specter of AIDS.

On one level, what they created was pure, unadulterated escape. No one on the floor of the Warsaw Ballroom that night cared one damn bit about sickness or death or the consequences of either. The macabre, pressed up against the joyous, created a force greater than its parts. Not to mention one hell of a party.

I'd been swept away that night, not only by the sheer intensity of the experience and the way it melded me to Rachael, but by the way I interpreted that intensity as profound, life-changing meaningfulness. That was saying something, considering I am about the least spiritual person I know. In my defense, my upbringing hadn't stressed the Holy Ghost. My mother had an icon depicting the Virgin Mary at her bedside table and kissed it dutifully every morning. But I never heard her speak of God. My father had grown up in a Seventh Day Adventist home, attended a Seventh Day Adventist high school and was primed to enter the seminary before he rejected the church all together. My grandparents occasionally dragged me to Easter mass at the Greek Orthodox Church. I remember the candles glowing underneath the immense stained-glass windows, the incantations performed in ancient Greek, and the pungent haze of the incense. Come to think of it, not all that different from a Saturday night in New York at the Limelight, a nightclub in Chelsea housed in the former site of the Episcopal Church of the Holy Communion. In the late eighties and early nineties, Limelight was ground zero for the Club Kid movement, the manifestation of disaffected youth who danced, did drugs, and dressed in enough spandex, vampire makeup, and platform shoes to make comic book illustrators and Broadway costume designers keel over with envy. As nightclubs go, Limelight was a pretty good mash-up of the holy and the profane.

Out on the dance floor of the Warsaw, though, I'd mainlined something and whatever the hell it was, I wanted more of it. And then, as if to seal the deal, there were a series of events which swept Rachael and I along in its rainbow-colored tidal surge. First, was the AIDS quilt, which visited Washington, D.C. in October of 1992. It was an awesome sight: a series of hand-made quilts, one for each dead friend or family member, patched together on the National Mall to form a fifteen-acre memorial. The event brought hundreds of thousands of people from all over the world to Washington. For several days, it was as though I was living in a never-before-aired segment of *The Twilight Zone* in which a straight man wakes to find that the entire world has turned homosexual. Gay people were everywhere. Packing the streets, hotel lobbies, restaurants, banks, and movie theaters. There were parades and marches and speeches condemning the first Bush administration for its inaction regarding the AIDS epidemic and international press coverage, some of which condemned those who were doing the condemning. But there was hope. The next presidential election would bring in a new era—ours. There were cocktail parties hosted by our friends and attended by gay people from everywhere, many of whom were feeling proud and hopeful for the first time in their lives.

Clinton won, and Rachael and I attended one of the inaugural parties, where we dressed in expensive clothes to sip cheap Chablis and watch our new president play the saxophone and dance with his wife, who was proclaimed by a lesbian comedienne to be the first First Lady in history she wanted to fuck.

Several months later, a huge gay-rights march ripped through Washington. We watched as the parade sashayed right down Constitution Avenue. There were marching bands, disco floats, leather daddies on Harleys, and topless lesbians. We partied at the Old Post Office, which was converted into a gigantic patriotic disco, complete with an enormous American flag, streamers, and go-go boys.

It was a time for change.

We began with our living arrangements. Rachael had walked away from most of the possessions she had accumulated with David. "New life, new stuff," she said. Even so, accommodating the two of us in my four-hundred square foot apartment was the equivalent of having to sit on an over-packed suitcase in order to latch it closed. Something had to give, and soon.

Within a few months, we'd found a pastel-colored Dutch Colonial row house over in Mt. Pleasant, an up-and-coming neighborhood just behind the National Zoo, and put down a deposit. It had five bedrooms, two fireplaces, a laundry room, full basement, a bricked patio, formal dining room and a kitchen with so many cabinets we would designate one just for pot lids.

As if that weren't enough, Rachael was considering a career change, too, something she said she'd thought about for years, something combining her two great passions—dogs and enterprise. Animals, dogs in particular, touched Rachael's soft spot. She had no maternal instinct. Hand her a baby to hold and she'd freeze, as if presented with a ticking bomb. A dog, however, even the mangiest stray, transformed her into a cooing, baby-talking softie.

"Think about it. Daycare for dogs," she said. "The Ritz for pets. They have them in LA and New York; it's just a matter of time before someone does it here. I'm telling you, it's the next big thing."

We'd gone as far as to scope out locations and had found a good one, across town on Capitol Hill, a defunct plumbing supply business with a large outdoor lot. Rachael was beside herself. "You can help me run it. Think about it. Our own business. I even have the name: Big Bark. It's perfect, right?"

I had to admit, it was. I'd never imagined myself a business owner. There was one big impediment: money. Rachael had some savings, but I wasn't working, we'd just bought a house, and here was Rachael talking about dumping her six-figure salary, plus benefits, to start a business no one in D.C. had ever hear of. Still, she seemed so sure, so absolutely sure. Who was I to argue? She had come along and rescued me. Now it was her turn to turn her life around and my turn to help her do it.

I don't recall who first brought up the prospect of getting married. I know that there was no formal proposal. Instead, we treated the event as just another in a series of changes to be planned and realized. The wedding would take place in January in New York City at the Plaza. Rachael knew the sales manager and she would cut us a deal. The guest list would be small, the ceremony Jewish. Only our closest friends would be invited. Parents would not.

As for the rest? Well, it would have to—as everything else seemed to be doing—fall into place.

Pre-Nuptials

A laser-like ray of late-afternoon sun angled through the enormous window behind us, struck the crystal chandelier hanging in the center of the room in which we would be married, and sprayed tiny, fractured rainbows everywhere. Rachael slid over to me and rested her head on my shoulder. I threaded her long, dark hair through my fingers. The marriage license had been procured, the menu selected, the piano player chosen. We'd just met with the cantor, who seemed perfectly okay with not mentioning God in the service.

"What did you make of him?" Rachael asked.

"He seemed nice. Especially after you wrote him that check."

"And you," she said. "What do you make of me?"

I kissed the top of her head, which smelled of jasmine. "An honest woman?"

"Best of luck. No, really. We're getting married."

"Right."

"Tomorrow. Here."

"I know."

Rachael sat bolt upright in her chair. "So you're getting married tomorrow, and you have nothing to say about it. Nothing to say about me?"

A year ago, none of this—the romance, the wedding, our friends—would have seemed possible. Rachael's hair was slightly disheveled from my playing with it. In a moment she would fix it, but right now it was untamed, a perfect counterpoint to her expertly applied makeup, burgundy cashmere sweater, and black wool pants. The chaos just beneath the control. I loved her. Not in the frothy, excited way I had loved before. This was what real love, the adult kind, must be.

I placed my hand under her chin and looked her in the eyes. "I don't quite know what to make of you." She tried to speak, but I squeezed her chin gently between my thumb and index finger. "But I know that you are the most remarkable person I've ever met."

I let go and she dabbed at her eyes with the tips of her fingers. She leaned over and kissed me. "You know how high maintenance I am."

"Yes."

"You know what a bitch I can be."

"Uh-huh."

"You know I adore you and that there's nothing I wouldn't do for you."

"Yep."

"I suppose that's full disclosure."

"One more thing. I've been meaning to ask you."

"About what?"

"All this. About me."

"What are you talking about?"

I shifted myself around to face her. "My world before you was small. Now, it's huge."

"So?"

"Sometimes I wonder if I'm big enough for it."

Rachael looked as though she might cry or laugh, or both. She slid over onto my lap. "Ask anyone. They'll tell you how lucky I am." She tugged my ear. "My job is to dream. Yours is to believe in the dream. Deal?"

"Deal."

Rachael leaned over, pulled a black comb out of her purse and began to fix her hair.

The wedding was, and remains, a blur. I remember a long table, beautifully decorated with glittering wine goblets, Rachael in her empire waisted dress, wearing jungle-red lipstick, which tasted waxy and sweet when I kissed her. I recall that the cantor had a lovely voice, redolent with vibrato, and that our friends dabbed their eyes with their napkins during the ceremony, which several of them missed because they were in the bathroom doing bumps of coke. I remember how the glass sounded like a finger snap when I stepped on it. And I recall a wizened couple snagging a couple of lamb chops before they asked if this was the Bernstein wedding. Most of all, I remember dancing with Rachael to Louis Armstrong's *What a Wonderful World* and thinking it was, it really was.

9

Toasted

Somehow, Rachael's friend, Sabrina, who was the sales director at the Plaza, finagled our way into Manhattan's club *du jour*, Bash. The fifty-dollar-a-head cover fee for our whole group was her wedding gift. We had commandeered a table on the far side of the dance floor, where Trevor stood and removed his hound's-tooth patterned Prada jacket carefully folding it over one of the armchairs. He corralled everyone into a semicircle and directed me and Rachael to stand in the center. I put my arm around Rachael's waist.

Trevor waited until he had everyone's attention. "I've been thinking all night about how to describe this event in my diary. I've decided that the word 'wedding' is too banal and doesn't do it justice." We nodded our heads, agreeing. "Other words describe it more accurately. Cotillion, bacchanal, coronation."

"Miracle," someone yelled.

Trevor smiled. "So, I've decided that there are certain events for which there simply aren't words. Just as there are certain people who defy description." Trevor looked at Rachael. "Fifteen year ago, I met a girl who worked with me at a crummy little clothing store in Wheaton, Maryland, the land of narrow horizons and low expectations. Rachael and I found a bond in the misery of being forced to grow up in such a place. From the day I met her, I knew that Rachael would never give in to Wheaton, that its gas stations and strip malls and provincial attitudes would never trap her. Every day, she'd come in with the latest issue of *Vogue* or the *Times,* and we'd talk about a glittering world where people accomplished things and lived important, meaningful lives. I've never doubted Rachael's ability to do whatever she sets her mind to, and the fact that we're here tonight makes my point as well as it can be made." He cleared his throat. "To Nick, whom I've known for a much shorter time, I can only say that you've got your hands full. But in you I think Rachael's found what we're all looking for in a man. Kindness, compassion, and a high ass." Everyone laughed. "My hope is that Nick will be, as I am, constantly amazed at Rachael's loyalty, her intellect, her passion and her ability to accessorize. Thank you, Rachael, for your love and friendship, and most of all, thank you for giving me an excuse to wear my new Prada suit." Trevor raised his glass high above his head. "May their love be like this toast. Endless."

Everyone downed champagne and let out a big cheer. Rachael walked over to Trevor, whispered something in his ear and they hugged. One by one, people came over to congratulate me. Suddenly, I felt exhausted. I walked over to a sofa and fell back into it, resting the back of my head between my intertwined fingers.

Trevor glanced over and sat down next to me.

"You okay?" he asked, putting his arm around me.

"Just taking it all in," I said. "That was a great toast. Thank you."

"You're welcome. I meant all of it. You make her happy."

Finally, I thought, here was the thaw I had been waiting for. "That's good to hear."

He squeezed my shoulder. "It takes a lot to make her happy. It'll take a lot more to keep her that way."

"Meaning what?"

Trevor shifted himself around, considering. "Sometimes, a customer will come into my restaurant, and I can tell right away they think they're slumming. They left New York for some big government appointment in D.C. and they've allowed their secretary to choose where she wants to go for her birthday. I used to pay special attention to those types. You know, give them the best server, made sure I stopped by the table to say hello. And then I realized that no matter what I did, no matter how good the food was, it wouldn't matter. It would never be good enough."

"So, Rachael is slumming in my restaurant?"

"I'm saying you're way out of your league."

I laughed. "Tell me something I don't know."

Trevor patted my shoulder, drew back his arm, stood and walked off, leaving me alone on the sofa, my grin fading to something else.

10

Gone to the Dogs

Trevor's comment at the wedding reception rocked me. It puzzled me, too. Was it a put down, a warning, or both? More importantly, was he right? Had all my efforts to fit in turned me into a poseur? I thought about telling Rachael what happened but decided against it. The last thing I wanted to be was the kid who ran in from recess to tell on the bully.

I didn't have much time to dwell on Trevor's pronouncement. A few days after Rachael returned to work, I received a call from a bawling, hysterical woman who claimed to be her. Turns out it was.

"I can't do this anymore," she said, between great gasping, blubbery sobs.

"What is *this*?" I asked.

"This job. These people."

This wasn't the first time I'd heard her spout off about work, the hours, the pressure, and the lack of respect. I'd never heard her quite this undone, though.

"So, do it," I said.

"Do what."

"Quit."

"Now?"

"Why not? We have the location, you have me. Now is the time."

She stopped crying.

A month later, we signed a lease for the space that would become Big Bark. What we got for the paltry sum of nine hundred a month was about a quarter acre of urban blight-meets-post-apocalyptic nightmare. Set at the end of a dead-end street, under the shadow of a highway overpass, our world headquarters, as we referred to it, had once been the home of a plumbing contractor. Abandoned for more than a decade, it had more recently played host to a cross-section of crack heads, junkies, hookers, and their johns. Still, the location gave us everything we needed: low overhead; an office attached to a large, indoor play/sleep area; several large shipping containers we could use for storage; a small, two-story federal-style house; and, most importantly, more than six-thousand square feet of outdoor space, which was plenty big enough for the twenty-five dogs we'd budgeted on to romp and play.

We worked twelve, often fourteen-hour days, clearing the lot—generously sprinkled with car tires, syringes and condoms—over which we spread two dump-truck loads of pea gravel. We erected a six-foot-high privacy fence around the perimeter of the property. Then came the endless cleaning; painting (periwinkle blue, the "it" color according to Rachael); trips to IKEA for office furniture, lighting, and storage bins; ordering merchandise, shelving, crates, and displays; designing the logo, and getting the necessary permits.

One morning, we were so worn out we could hardly move. But we had to finish painting the bathroom before the plumbers showed up the next day. Rachael produced a little baggie of white powder and tossed it on the desk.

"Here," she said, scooping out a tiny bit. "A gift from Wes."

Not so long ago, I wouldn't have even known what crystal meth was, much less considered doing it. But crystal, formerly known as crank, a moniker derived from biker gangs' habit of stashing it in the crankcases of their Harleys, was making a big comeback, especially in the gay community. Two bumps and you were good to go—and go and go. How else were you supposed to get through a circuit party weekend, which often meant going flat out for three or four days on just a few hours of sleep? How else could you (as some of our friends were doing) head up to New York on a Friday, check into the West Side Club, rent a room, stash your clothes in a locker and have at it with half of Chelsea until Monday morning?

Call her what you will: Tina, mother's little helper, Chrissie, ice, the girl—when it came to getting things done, she could be a miracle. We blasted right through the painting, hardly needed to sleep, had to remind ourselves to eat. That little baggie and the ubiquitous blue Bic-pen cap became an essential tool in getting Big Bark off the ground. When Trevor found out, he warned us about the temptation to do crystal to get through the day, how it was a slippery slope and a trap. Rachael wasn't worried. She'd been able to manage her cocaine use for years. We made a rule—no crystal at work—then frequently broke it.

Six weeks of flat-out effort and Big Bark was ready. By doing much of the work ourselves, we had gotten Big Bark ready to open on a shoestring budget. Still, we'd sunk nearly $20,000 into the business, almost everything we had. Reluctantly, Rachael decided to approach her father for a loan to give us some operating capital. Besides, she said, it was time I met the in-laws. Over a long lunch at our house, I did.

Her father, a retired statistician, was slender, intense and bore a distinct resemblance to Marty Feldman, right down to the bulging eyes, one of which wandered. Despite an abysmal medical history that included several heart attacks and various forms of cancer—conditions, according to Rachael, which were directly attributable to a lifetime of rage—his mind was astonishingly sharp. Her mother was docile, earnest and, in her mid-seventies, still beautiful, with the pale, translucent and unblemished skin of a young woman.

With her father, Rachael was solicitous but guarded. With her mother, abrupt and dismissive. With me, her parents were unfailingly polite and, despite the way Rachael had portrayed them, surprisingly warm. After producing four daughters, they must have welcomed a jolt of testosterone in the family. Try as I might, I couldn't imagine these people as Rachael had portrayed them: the union of a monstrous tyrant and a self-centered martyr. I took to them immediately, a turn of events which seemed to irk Rachael, as though by warming to her parents I was disrupting the continuity of her carefully constructed family narrative. Strangely enough, by liking my in-laws I felt as though was also betraying my wife.

After lunch, the four of us sat in the parlor as Rachael went over the spreadsheet projections for the business. Her father asked plenty of questions. Her mother sipped her espresso quietly.

A couple of days later, her father got back to Rachael with his verdict. He had serious doubts about the viability of the business. He would lend us the money, but only under certain strict conditions.

Rachael was furious. She'd always made her own way, never asked her father for a thing, and now, instead of trusting her, he was throwing up tons of obstacles. This was it. She was writing them off. "Cutting them out of my life like a cancer." I sat quietly as she stormed around the house screaming and sobbing.

Now, the pressure was really on. We had to have positive cash flow within six months or we'd be knee deep in dog shit. We considered several marketing strategies and settled on one featuring two powerful motivators: snobbery and shame. Instead of the conventional business tactic of offering a new service at a rock-bottom price to entice customers, we did just the opposite. We set the price high: twenty dollars a day for daycare, thirty-five for overnight boarding. In order to play up the exclusivity of the service, we developed an application process, including a comprehensive, five-page questionnaire each owner had to complete before their dog would be considered Big Bark material.

Rachael contacted every local media outlet and pitched the angle. They loved it: "Pampered Pooches Put on Airs at New DC Pet Hotel," read one headline. News crews stacked up outside to do live remotes. We ran an ad in the local papers featuring a black and white photo of a scraggly terrier, his eyes pleading, his ears pinned back pathetically. Underneath, it read, "Guilty about leaving me home all day?"

Finally, by the fall of 1998, everything was clean and organized and ready. A part of me, the compulsively neat and organized part, wished it could stay just this way, with a nice spacious yard, a modern office, and a play area that looked like Romper Room. But, of course, we had to open.

And when we did, we opened big. Customers included workaholic attorneys, lobbyists, ladies who lunch, tourists, all willing to spend serious money on their dogs. Perhaps we were smart, but we were also lucky. The economy surged, people started moving back into the city, the housing and stock market boomed, and Big Bark was a home run. Our first month, we covered our expenses. The next month, we turned a profit. A few months later we took a chance and raised our prices fifteen percent. Business surged. Initially, we figured it might take us up to a year to attract twenty-five dogs a day. It took two months. Soon, we were up to an average of thirty dogs, with many more than that over holidays.

The first months we were in business remain a hazy memory. We had no staff and plenty of customers, many of whom began using us immediately for overnight boarding. We moved a small fold-out couch into the office and slept there, often surrounded by a dozen or more snoring dogs. Our friends contributed to the effort in ways which, to this day, move me. The first Christmas Eve after we opened Big Bark, Rachael and I were stuck boarding the dogs for the holidays. We were paid an unexpected visit by Trevor and Wes dressed in Santa outfits and bearing a complete roast turkey feast. After dinner, we lounged on dog beds around the office and watched the Charlie Brown Christmas special, the story line enhanced by bumps of Wes' ketamine.

Very quickly, Rachael and I fell into roles which were governed somewhat by our skills, but more so our temperaments. I was better with the new clients, with whom Rachael could be direct to a fault. So, I did most of the customer intakes, sitting down with the clients in the office to answer questions and fill in the customer profile, while their dog was out in the exercise area being assessed by Rachael. Some new customers were reluctant to part with their pooches. But once I broke the news to perspective clients that there were certain prerequisites to admission, such as temperament, which meant that Hubert, the German shorthaired pointer, for which they had paid a king's ransom and fed only ground sirloin and diced organic carrots, wasn't guaranteed admittance to Big Bark, they began acting like parents trying to score a slot in an Ivy League college. They would say *anything*. More than once, a dog which the owner had characterized as Scooby-Doo, would break out into a snarling impersonation of Cujo. I heard more excuses for unruly behavior than the parole commission at the federal penitentiary.

The dogs we could handle. It was the customers who could be incorrigible, demanding special treatment and kid gloves. Patience, charm, and efficiency eventually won their trust and their loyalty, which paid off in the form of checks for services rendered which often exceeded the mortgage payment on our house.

If I was good with the paying customers, then Rachael was even better with the four-legged ones. She was a born pack leader, tough but fair, just like John Wayne. Whether she was dealing with a two-hundred-pound mastiff or a four-pound Maltese, the relationship was the same—mutual respect bordering on mutual adoration. I can still picture her out in the exercise yard, tromping through the gravel with a Frisbee or a tennis ball, followed closely by a pack of twenty dogs of every conceivable shape and size, or on the phone in the office, with a dog sound asleep in her lap and ten more spread out on the floor around her like area rugs. It's hard to say who was happier.

Six months after we opened, we hired a manager. Anna was a fifty-something, no-nonsense Swiss divorcee who looked like Nurse Ratched from *One Flew Over the Cuckoo's Nest,* but had a better bedside manner. For years, she'd managed her ex-husband's veterinary clinic. Customers loved her and so did we. We fixed up the little house on the Big Bark property and Anna moved in as Big Bark's resident manager.

We had ourselves a successful business. And, for the first time, I saw the way that desire, work, and vision could be transformed into success. Who knew? Rachael, that's who.

11

Family Matters

Not long after we opened Big Bark, my mother paid us a congratulatory visit, her first to our house. Given their predilection for the company of gay men, my mother and Rachael should have been close. They weren't. My mother felt Rachael was cold and distant. Rachael felt my mother was needy and intrusive. They both had a point.

Rachael, who had done everything she could to distance herself from her family, saw little value in mine. Convinced that, given the opportunity, my family would insinuate itself into our lives and threaten the world that she was building for us, Rachael met my mother's attempts to connect with her with an emotional stiff-arm. My mother, who had been close with the other women in my life, couldn't understand why Rachael couldn't behave like a proper member of the family.

That afternoon, my mother brought along her closest friend, Larry. Larry was a hairdresser, about Rachael's height, with a physique to match his pencil-thin mustache. Larry arrived with a spray of white roses in one arm, my mother in the other. They wandered from one room to the next, amazed and overwhelmed by the size of the house, easily four times the size of anywhere my mother and I ever lived. Standing in our dining room, Larry was overcome. "It's all so beautiful. Sssstunning. Th-imply sssstunning," he said, dabbing his eyes with a tissue. He presented Rachael the roses with much greater flourish and formality than even I, the former tuxedo-clad flower delivery man, could ever muster. Rachael was gracious, if not warm.

After they left, Rachael stood there, holding her roses and leaning with her back against the door.

"That wasn't so bad," I said.

"No, it wasn't. Which is how you're going to feel when you meet David."

"Your ex?"

Rachael nodded.

My expression must have said what I was thinking.

"Come on, Nick. He was as much a part of my life as any family member. More, actually."

Rachael had been pressing me to meet David for months. She insisted that his anger over being dumped had dissipated to the point he'd admitted to Rachael that, romantically at least, it had been over between them long ago. No hard feelings. He'd moved on, even begun dating again. In fact, in a gesture of generosity that even she found surprising, David paid Rachael back some of the money she'd invested in their house. I resisted. No matter how you spun it, there was no disputing that I had come to his house, snorted up a bunch of his cocaine, and stolen his woman. Guys had been knifed and left in alleys to bleed to death for less. Hell, in certain cultures, being knifed and left to bleed in an alley for what I had done would be considered an act of restraint.

I glanced down at the bunch of roses Larry had presented Rachel, so large they nearly obscured her.

"Do I get a say in this?"

Her smile answered my question.

"When?" I asked.

"I was thinking tomorrow evening."

By inviting my mother, I had stepped right into Rachael's bear trap. "Okay, Ms. Tit-For-Tat. I'll meet Mr. Quid Pro Quo."

Rachael tugged on one of my earlobes. "You can just call him David." She shot by me wafting the thick scent of roses, already headed to the phone.

12

Disco Boy meets the Ex

The next evening arrived too soon. I recall several costume changes on my part, spiraling down in formality from *meet the in-laws*, to *business casual Friday*, to *company picnic*, to *swing by the grocery store*, and, finally, what I thought struck the right balance, somewhere between hip and menacing: *street hustler*, which consisted of torn jeans and a cobalt blue tank top.

The doorbell rang, Rachael answered and there he was, looking pretty much as he had in the photos I'd seen of him on the mantlepiece in their living room, handsome, with a broad, open smile, a nearly shaved head, dressed casually in jeans and a polo shirt. Lacoste to my International Male.

David had brought along the dogs, the ultimate ice breakers. When Rachael saw Sallie and Dusty, she nearly collapsed. The next several minutes were spent in a joyous reunion. I'm not sure who did more panting and squealing, the dogs or Rachael.

I expected our meeting would be cordial, but I'd also prepared myself for the possibility of some sword crossing. But when David crossed the vestibule, ignored my outstretched hand, and hugged me, my anxiety took a hike. As soon as we all settled in the parlor, David produced a vial of coke and set it on the coffee table.

"One thing she taught me," David said to me,

"never show up empty handed."

"I think I taught you more than that," Rachael said. "His artwork consisted of framed *Sports Illustrated* covers."

"Guilty," David said.

"Then, there was the matter of your clothes."

"True enough." He turned to me. "I have emerged a thoroughly re-made man. Highly evolved. I'm all the way up to Cro-Magnon."

The thing that impressed me most about David was the way his self-deprecation also managed to convey his confidence. It didn't hurt that his cocaine was excellent. The rest of the evening went beautifully. In fact, when Rachael excused herself to fill a water bowl for the dogs, David and I waved her off like a couple of kids pretending to be sorry that their mother had to leave.

"I've got to tell you something." I freshened up his drink with some vodka and handed it to him. "Now that I meet you, I just don't get it."

He took a swallow. "Get what?"

"Why she left you."

David leaned back in the sofa and crossed his legs. "Oh hell, neither one of us wanted to admit it, but things had gotten pretty stale. It was for the best. You know how I know that?"

I shook my head.

"She's happy. If she had been like this with me, I'd have fought you for her." He swirled his drink around in the glass. "I heard about that time you had in Miami Beach. She thought I was too old for that kind of stuff. Not that she ever asked me."

"And if she had?"

He shrugged. "Guess we'll never know."

David had given me an idea. My immersion into gay life had been a solo effort. I never imagined there was another straight man out there who might share the experience. But here he was, sitting not three feet away. Hobnobbing with the boys was a minimum prerequisite for any sort of relationship with Rachael. According to Rachael, David had a homo-friendly history that pre-dated her, including coaching an all-girl softball team. And, unlike me, David had dabbled with men at least once when she, David, and two friends had spent a drunken, coked-out evening fumbling around, groping each other on the sofa and rolling across the living room floor. Drugs certainly weren't an issue. David had grown up in the sixties. He was getting high when I was still sipping Hi-C.

"Hey, listen. We're headed up to New York in a few weeks for this S&M, circuit thing. Why don't you come?"

David pursed his lips skeptically. "You don't want me in tow."

"I'm telling you, what happened to me down in Miami? It was something special, man. Who knows, might stir up some stray hot girls decked out in leather."

He thought for a moment, set his cocktail down on a coaster, then leaned forward and snorted a line of coke.

"What do you say?" I asked. "Old man."

David pinched his nostrils and smiled. "Can't say I'm not curious."

"Then it's yes?"

He winked at me. "You're on, Disco Boy."

Rachael walked back into the room, took one look at us, and stopped cold. "What?"

"He," I pointed to David, "called me Disco Boy."

Rachael started to say something. "And he is going with us to the Black Party."

Rachael put her hands on her hips. "You're kidding."

"Right on both accounts," David said.

"You never wanted to do anything like this before."

"You never asked," he said.

Rachael swung around to me. "And all this was decided while I was away for five minutes?"

"Yep," I said.

Rachael sat on the sofa next to David. "You're not going to have a problem with a bunch of leather daddies with their asses hanging out?"

"That would depend on the asses," David said.

Rachael stood there, considering. Finally, she nodded. "Long as you know what you're in for."

Of course, we didn't.

13

Punch Drunk

Trevor was not physically imposing. However, clad in a gladiator skirt, a shirt resembling a chain link fence, and a ton of attitude, he was a force. It was Trevor who had cleared a path for us in Roseland Ballroom's sweltering coat-check room, Trevor who had scored bottles of water from the packed bar. Since our wedding, I had gone out of my way to avoid him. His attitude towards me seemed unchanged: aloof tolerance, which I did my best to reflect right back at him.

Finally, we were on the dance floor, cocooned in the crowd, and locked into the music. Deejay David Knapp was hitting it just right with a thick and thunderous groove. In response, we had formed a joyous little circle, which shrank and expanded to accommodate whoever happened to pass by and latch on. At that moment, it was comprised of a very tall man from LA who had both long arms draped around Rachael; two brawny lesbians attached to each other at the collar by a dog leash who glared at me and David like hungry wolves; and a couple of bears sporting bushy beards like mountain men. I put my hand on David's shoulder and turned him to face me. His eyes were at quarter-mast.

Whatdya' think?" I asked.

David pursed his lips. "I gotta' say," he pointed

right and left with his index fingers, "this part doesn't suck."

A magnificent wave of ecstasy-borne delight surged through me. I was bursting with chemically induced inquisitiveness and the need to connect. "I'm curious about something."

"What's that?"

"Do you miss her?"

"Rachael?" David cocked his head and looked past me for a moment, thinking. "She makes you feel like the world's an inside joke and only you and she get it. That part I miss." He shook his head. "Then, there's the part that's so dark and scared." He clamped his hands together. "She can suck the life right out of life."

I'd seen vulnerability in Rachael. In her job, after she left David. In fact, I found that vulnerability one of her most appealing traits. But I hadn't considered that she may have framed her entire life around one organizing principle, that life was a house of cards.

"All the extremes," David said. "That's how she lets go without really having to let go."

"*Controlled* substances," I said.

"Bingo."

I was seized by the image of David, brought back by Rachael to the customer service counter, somewhere in the bowels of a high-end department store.

"This one doesn't really work for me anymore," says Rachael to the clerk.

"I'm so sorry," the clerk says. "What seems to be the problem?"

Rachael turns and regards David. "He's starting to wear out. I need something younger. More obedient."

The clerk smiles. "I completely understand. I think

we have just what you're looking for." She leaves for a moment, then reappears leading me along by my ear. "This is our latest model. Young, easy on the eyes, docile, lost, eager to please." The clerk turns and looks me up and down. "They're literally flying off the shelf."

"I'll take him," says Rachael. "No need to wrap. I'll wear him out."

The clerk smiles. "Oh, I'm sure you will."

Their laughter jarred me back to the present.

Over David's shoulder I spotted an area curtained off by ominous looking black drapes. "Hey," I leaned in to make myself heard over the music, "want to see what goes on behind that curtain?"

"Like *Let's Make a Deal*?"

"I doubt it. You game?"

David put an arm over my shoulder and smiled. He licked his lips. "Abso-fucking-lutely."

Rachael gave us a suspicious look. "What are you two up to?"

"We're going to check out the sex-position."

"That is probably a terrible idea."

"What's the big deal?" David said.

In the best horror-movie tradition, Rachael's creations were challenging their creator. The idea to invite David here had been genius. It was paying off in ways I hadn't even imagined.

"Okay," she said. She slid her still-cold water bottle across David's forehead. "But don't come back here with your tails, or anything else, between your legs."

"Oh *please*," I said, "what haven't we seen before?"

"Plenty," Trevor said. "I just passed a guy with jumper cables attached to his nipples."

In her serious voice, Rachael said, "You guys have

to remember how to find us. Right here under the disco ball, okay? *Okay?*" she said, squeezing my hands hard.

"Under the disco ball. Is that a Merchant Ivory film?" David asked.

He and I looked at each other and burst out laughing.

Rachael waved us off. "Hope you both come back with a good case of chlamydia."

And so, with my arm draped around David and both of us tittering like nine-year-olds who sneaked into the movie theater, we made our way across the dance floor and around the curtain.

In an eerie half-light, hundreds of men milled around, waiting in front of a stage that was empty save for one folding chair. We positioned ourselves to get the best view. Five minutes passed. David threw me a so-what's-the-big-deal look. I threw it right back at him. *How should I know?*

David turned to the man standing to his left, a very tall, very pale, very thin, skinhead-meets-Iggy Pop type. "So, what goes on here?" he asked.

"One never quite knows," he said in a British accent.

"I heard the shows can get pretty heavy," I said.

"Actually, I'd say they're spot-on," he said, smiling. His two canines jutted forward, like a vampire's.

A very muscular man, square-jawed with salty-gray close-cropped hair, wearing tight black chaps, crisscross harness, and a black leather short-brimmed hat, mounted the stage and stood next to the chair. The man inserted each thick finger of his hands into a pair of surgical gloves, rolled them down over his palms to his wrists and gave each one a loud *snap*. Then, he took a toothpaste-like tube from the chair and squeezed a clear, viscous liquid down each hand. The excess dripped onto the floor of the riser.

"Oh my," said Iggy-skinhead.

David juked me with his elbow. "Can't be good."

"What?"

"Vlad the Impaler here just said 'Oh my.'"

A thin, olive-skinned man—baby-faced, naked and hairless—walked onto the riser. A smattering of applause spread through the crowd, but so did a nervous buzz. The boy bent forward, resting his palms on the seat of the chair.

Someone tapped me on my shoulder. Iggy-skinhead had his arm around David's waist. He leaned over and said to me, "I think your friend is having a bit of a problem."

David had gone bleached-bone white, except for the dark bruise-like circles which had formed perfect half-moons under his eyes. Beads of sweat dotted his forehead, dripping down his cheeks and off the end of his chin.

"Get me out of here," he said.

I put my arm across David's back to support him and we slowly threaded our way back out of the exposition area and over to a quiet spot in the far corner. We leaned back against the wall and slid down onto our haunches.

After a few moments, he said, "Sorry."

"Don't be. I was right behind you. So to speak," I added.

"Funny. One thing's for sure."

"What's that?"

"I've had my last prostate exam."

"Amen, brother."

He turned to me. "Know what the worst thing is?"

"What?"

"Rachael was right."

14

The Waiting Game

I n retrospect, the Black Party wasn't anyone's best induction into the circuit. Unlike other events, which were cheery themed and inclusive, often attended by dabblers and straight women out to have fun with their gay friends, the Black Party was, well, black. A testosterone-filled freak-fest. The sadomasochistic theme wasn't all for show. Beyond the outfits, decorations and other external trappings, there was a palpable feeling of the down-and-dirty out to play. The hardcore guys came here, men who enjoyed rough, primal, painful sex. If you hooked up with one of them, you'd better not forget the safe word, or risk ending up like one of our friends: blindfolded with duct tape and hogtied, getting slapped around and violated, all the while crying, his pleas interpreted by his dates as encouragement.

For most men, gay or straight, the scene was too intense. I, on the other hand, returned from the Black Party feeling as though a veil had been lifted. Or in this case a rubber bondage mask with little air holes cut into it. Up until now, I had let Rachael take the lead regarding all the major decisions in our life. A strong woman in charge of things was all I knew. Now, I began to recognize that Rachael's effort to control me along with everything else, was, as David had pointed out, based in fear, not strength.

Strangely, I saw the circuit, the gayest scene in the whole world, as a pathway to a new, more powerful me. Apart from whipping up my self-esteem, I began to see the parties as a kind of primal initiation ceremony. Urged on by the dark, relentless music, the lights, the drugs, and the men, dancing on and on for hours to the point of exhaustion and pushing past it, I imagined myself part of a ritual stretching back through time, when hunters celebrated around a gigantic bonfire celebrating a massive kill. Sure, some of it was too much. Case in point, the fisting demonstration that had sent David and I packing. But didn't most male initiation rituals involve mental and physical challenges, tests of bravery, and the requirement to face one's fears?

My attraction to the circuit wasn't based solely on a high-minded quest for enlightenment. There was another motivating, and unexpected, factor. Females were rare in the circuit, which was, as far as Rachael was concerned, just fine by her. In a world dominated by men, she was the pretty, profane anomaly. There did exist, however, a small but significant cadre of girls who partied like, and with, the boys.

There were lots of flirtations and quite a few near misses: the Latina nurse at Liquid in Miami Beach who led Rachael and me to a quiet part of the club and behaved like she meant it—until she didn't; the blonde/brunette couple who sandwiched me between them for hours at Trevor and Wes's New Year's Eve party, whispering what they had in mind, until they pulled the lifeline and floated safely and chastely to earth; the diminutive and adorable mortician who made it all the way to our bedroom before, at the last possible moment, her blood turned to embalming fluid.

All this may sound like a free for all, but there were rules. Rachael's. Some were implicit. I knew better than take the point position in either the quest or the seduction, which would make her jealous, feel threatened, or both. Rachael made it clear that the pursuit of these girls was a joint venture. Whatever we did, it would be done together, as a couple. Finally, these were to be one-night stands. There would be no attachments, and no follow up.

Notwithstanding the elaborate rule book, I regarded this aspect of our relationship as a boon. Unlike the average married *schlub*, I didn't have to feign disinterest in attractive women or sneak down to the basement with videos to indulge my fantasies. I figured that all I had to do was be patient, sit back, and wait. Eventually, someone would come along.

Her name was Trudie.

15

Home Run

I sat shirtless on the sofa in our parlor, my head resting on Wes's shoulder as we both watched Rachael seduce the only other woman in a house chock full of gay men. The object of Rachael's attention, Trudie, an abundantly-tattooed-thirty-something with a pageboy haircut and cherubic lips drawn into a perpetual pout, lay flat on her back on the floor just a few feet away from us. Rachael, wearing a white-leather studded bra and patent-leather hot pants, kneeled over her and carefully tapped out a small dollop of crystal from a glass vial onto the girl's bare stomach.

Half-naked men were everywhere, bathed in candlelight, in and out of the bathroom, drifting down the stairs from our bedrooms, laughing, flirting. It was Sunday morning, smack in the middle of D.C.'s Pride celebration. Following the parade, everyone had ended up at TRAX, where, as usual, closing time had arrived like a big, bright nightmare. We invited a few people over to our house, forgetting that news of an after party among a bunch of desperate club-goers could spread with the efficiency of fiber optics. Pretty soon, people we didn't know were coming up to us to ask if we were headed to Nick and Rachael's house. We managed to beat the crowd home, where Rachael and I ran around creating the mood: lowering lights, lighting candles, filling the CD player with a gentle, throbbing mix, and setting up a bar. Now, it was nearly dawn, and sex, or at least the possibility of it, floated through the party like a caressing mist.

Earlier, I'd done two hits of weak X, which had all but worn off. Usually, I'd gulp down a smoothie, excuse myself and head to bed, leaving Rachael to play hostess. Instead, I was glued to the sofa, my heart battering my chest like a bighorn sheep in rutting season.

Trudie giggled. "That tickles."

"Think that's funny?" said Rachael. She threw a knee over the girl and straddled her. "Hold back my hair." Their lips were so close they almost touched. Trudie smiled, flashing dimples, and gathered Rachael's long, dark hair up in her hands. Wispy strands of Rachael's hair flowed between Trudie's fingers, brushing over her cheek and neck.

"Face like a movie star," said Trudie.

"Which one?" Rachael asked.

Trudie squinted, studying Rachael a moment more. "You're Scarlet O'Hara," she said, proud of herself. "Look just like her. Small, but put together. Those eyes. The little waist. Without the accent, of course. Or the hoop skirt."

Rachael frowned.

Trudie looked confused. "I say something wrong? I thought everyone loves Scarlet O'Hara."

"Not at all, darling," Rachael said. "Scarlet was lovely. A little shrill. A bit needy. Manipulative." Wes and I laughed. "Oh, shut up, you two," she said.

Rachael turned back to Trudie, lowered her head slightly and slid her lips past the girl's. "Who would *you* like me to be, Trudie dear?" she said in a husky whisper.

Trudie stopped smiling and blinked three times, the importance of her response now apparent. "Well," she said, tentatively, "I did have this massive crush on that British chick on that old TV spy show." She looked past Rachael, thinking. "You know, black leather and judo?" She pursed those thick, red, button-shaped lips, and furrowed her forehead.

Wes grinned, turn his head slightly, and said into my ear, "That was a home run."

"Could still curve foul," I said.

Rachael arched her eyebrows. "Dianna Riggs in *The Avengers*." She took two fingers and tapped them against Trudie's lips. "Right answer," she said. "Now, stop worrying. You just sit back and let Ms. Peele take over."

Trudie obeyed. Rachael leaned over and drew the tip of her tongue very slowly down the girl's neck, past her small, bare, silver hoop-pierced breasts, down the flat of her stomach, past the little mound of white powder. Using her teeth, she undid the top snap of Trudie's jeans, exposing a small tattoo of a scorpion, claws up, stinger coiled. Rachael smiled as though she had been reunited with an old friend, kissed each claw, then gave the stinger a little bite. Trudie let out a low moan and arched her back. Rachael slid her lips back up Trudie's stomach, sniffed the powder, and traced her mouth around the girl's belly button.

"Not giggling now, are you?" said Rachael, resting her head on Trudie's stomach.

"She's playing her like a piano," Wes said.

"Bravo, maestro," I whispered.

"I'm going to go out on a limb here, straight guy," said Wes, handing me the baggie with the K, "and suppose that you're enjoying all this."

I took the baggie, tapped some on to my wrist. "You think?" I said, then bent forward and bumped. "Thanks." I handed it back to him.

"Who is she?"

"Rachael."

"Smart ass."

"Trudie. Manages an art gallery up in Baltimore," I said. "She just broke up with her girlfriend and came down to drown her sorrows."

"Doing a pretty good job." He leaned back and draped his arms across the top of the sofa. The beads woven into his braided extensions clacked together. Wes was engaged in perpetual conflict with his hair, careening from one style to the next: peroxide blond and buzz-cut, jet-black and shoulder length, and, the latest, Bo Dereck and braided.

"So, nothing about this situation appeals to you? Not even a little?" I said, holding my thumb and index finger close together.

"Wouldn't say that," Wes said. "It's more nostalgic than sexy. I used to be married to a woman, remember?"

"Speaking of which, where's that husband of yours?"

Wes motioned up toward the ceiling. "In one of your bedrooms, I expect. Entertaining or being entertained."

"And here you sit with me, watching the girls."

"The boys aren't going anywhere. Plus," he said, lowering his voice, "I need to see how this plays out."

"Listen." I squirmed. "I have to ask you something. Was there a time, like maybe the first time, when you felt, you know, like maybe you didn't know if, you know, how you'd do?"

Wes leaned back and looked me over. "I thought two girls was *it* for you dudes."

"It is."

"So, what's the problem?"

"I'm feeling the pressure."

He poked my arm with his finger. "You could at least wait for the performance to get the performance anxiety."

"Don't you guys ever have trouble?"

"It's different with boys. Besides, if we can't give, we can always receive."

I stared at the floor. "Forgot about that."

Rachael took Trudie's nipple ring between her teeth and gave it a tug. "Ow!" said Trudie.

I said, "I want to *want* to, not to have to. You know what I mean?"

"It's too late and I'm too high to know what you mean. All I know is that you had better want to have to, and soon."

Rachael said, "What in the world could you two be talking about that would be more interesting than this?"

"She's got a point," Wes said.

"My turn," Trudie said.

Rachael sat back on her haunches. "I have a better idea." She patted the floor next to Trudie.

My heart raced. "Me?"

"Brother, you are *on*," Wes said.

"Interesting," said Trudie, squinting. She got up to her knees and joined Rachael. There they sat smiling like silent sirens.

Wes shoved me with his elbow. "That's as close to a green light as you're going to get."

"I thought gay men were supposed to be so sensitive."

"Not when it comes to this." I leaned forward to get up, but Wes caught my forearm. "One more thing."

"What?" I said, annoyed.

"There's ground up Viagra in the K." Wes pinched my cheek. "Who loves ya', baby?"

My heart pounding like a bass drum, I slid off the sofa and lay down on my back between Rachael and Trudie, cradling my head in my intertwined fingers.

Rachael handed Trudie the vial. "Here, you do it."

Trudie bent over my chest. "How much?" she asked. I could smell her hair, the sweat from all the dancing and underneath that, a hint of something sweet and pungent as pomegranate.

Rachael took her hand and shook it. "Just enough."

I felt the powder collect on my sternum. Gentle music throbbed and pulsed as my heart found the rhythm and locked in. The edges of the room blurred and underneath me, the floor rocked.

Rachael took Trudie's other hand and began working it up and down my chest, across my stomach. "Quite the little alchemist, isn't she?" I said to Trudie.

"Don't know what an alchemist is," she said, "but if it means somebody used to getting their way, yes she is."

Rachael smiled.

"Haven't felt a man this way in a long time," Trudie said, watching her hand being directed up and down.

"It's like riding a bicycle," Rachael said. "You just let go," she released Trudie's hand, "and your body," she leaned over and nibbled Trudie's earlobe, "somehow, it does the rest."

Trudie paused a moment, then glided all ten fingernails across my chest. I broke out in goose bumps.

"You shave your chest?" Trudie asked.

"No, I wax," Rachael said.

Trudie snickered. "You remind me a little of my ex. A gorgeous smart ass." She reached down and undid the top two buttons of my jeans.

I looked over at Wes in mock surprise. He winked.

A couple of men headed from the bathroom to the kitchen looked down and stopped dead in their tracks. Trudie pressed her hand under my jeans a few more inches. Horizontal slivers of wan early morning light slipped through the blinds and played across the women's faces. Rachael's and Trudie's lips press together, twisted, parted, then rejoined.

"Don't forget about this," Rachael said, tapping my chest just next to the crystal, "Or this," she said, pressing on Trudie's hand, moving it down.

"I hadn't," Trudie said. "I won't." I felt her hot breath against the base of my neck.

There was a quick rush of air on my chest, replaced by something warm, then wet. I closed my eyes. A sizzling, crimson ball of light spun and sparked, drew in on itself, then exploded into jagged shards. When I opened my eyes, there was Rachael, looking down on me, smiling. She held her little finger out, a shiny red nail just over my nostril. "Here." There was the burn, followed by a rush and a pang. Whatever misgivings I had had just immolated. In their place was desire, urgent and searing hot.

I got up and placed my hands under both their arms, drawing them to me. "Ladies, shall we?"

"Yeah. Like, immediately," Trudie said, rubbing my chest with one hand, Rachael's back with the other. "Before the lesbo gene kicks in."

"Here, here," Wes said, clapping.

16

The Glitter Dome

The story of my life seemed to be in the hands of an author with a fondness for happy endings. Big Bark continued its surge. A year after we opened, we were averaging nearly fifty dogs a day. Demand for the boarding business was particularly strong, especially on holidays and in the summer, when one big weekend could make our month. The business was now generating a ten-to-fifteen-thousand-dollar-a-month profit—three times what we initially expected. By now, Anna was handling many of the day-to-day duties, including managing a staff of four full and part-time employees. We continued to spend a lot of time on-site, and success brought with it other responsibilities, such as bookkeeping and payroll. But we were no longer tethered to the place as we had been.

It should have come as no surprise to me that the rapid and grand success of Big Bark would give Rachael equally grand ideas. If Big Bark could garner enough press coverage and a strong enough reputation, we might be able to expand the company regionally, even nationally. These were boom times, the peak of the stock market and dot-com bubbles. Forward thinking companies such as AOL were establishing huge corporate headquarters, campuses really, all around D.C. In a time when just about everyone who wanted a job had one, companies were falling all over themselves to keep their employees happy by offering new benefits: childcare, fitness facilities, dry cleaning. Why not doggie daycare?

My acceptance into Rachael's world, the acquisition of our new house, all our new friends—even our encounter with Trudie—shoved my confidence level into orbit somewhere above the ionosphere. For the first time, I developed something approaching a swagger. Trevor's suggestion that I was over my head seemed ridiculous. I had more than proven myself.

I grew my hair down to my shoulders, got an arm-band tattoo in the pattern of a Greek key and, in the manner of many of our friends, shaved my chest. I hit the gym—hard—often in the company of one of our gym-rat friends, who showed me state-of-the-art routines designed to get the maximum bang for the buck in the places that count most: shoulders, abs, chest, and arms. We compiled a wish list of the most popular and exotic parties and planned our social lives around an ever-expanding list of events.

We were not alone. The circuit scene was exploding. Every month, there were more parties in more places. There was even a publication, *Circuit Noise*, with splashy ads for upcoming parties, featuring lasers, disco balls, and half-naked men, containing hard-hitting, incisive exposés with titles such as, "The Party Diet: back out the carbs and jack up the fun!"

First up was the Black and Blue Party in Montreal. Rachael, Trevor, Wes, and I joined twelve thousand people under the same enormous roof that hosted the Expos and made the Warsaw Ballroom in Miami Beach look like someone's spare bedroom. Cirque du Soleil performers and bungee jumpers dropped from the ceiling; deejay Junior Vasquez soaked the whole place down with his beats and then wrung us out like a dishrag. We met boys from Boston, New York, San Francisco, Chicago, London, and Australia. The Black and Blue drew hip, attractive people from all of Canada, including gorgeous French-Canadian women who wore nothing but spray paint and glitter and were invariably named Genevieve. Our hotel became a dorm, our doors flung open all the time, the party rolling from one room the next.

Then, there was New York for the gay pride celebration. We stayed with Dr. Hector at his place in the heart of Chelsea. Hector was quite the host, supremely attentive. In fact, he never seemed to sleep or eat. One day, the laconic deejay that Hector had hired and installed in his loft, played, with the assistance of Hector's meth, an uninterrupted twelve-hour set. I, wanting to be a good guest, ended up dancing on the coffee table for much of it.

Four years after our first visit, we returned to South Beach, which had been busy transforming itself into the hippest place on the planet. A group of us had dinner at the Delano hotel, amid the surreal Phillipe Starke designed, gauze-draped lobby and the Alice-in-Wonderland inspired oversized chess pieces out by the pool. In the bathroom, I urinated next to Jack Nicholson, who was looking *so* Jack Nicholson in his gray, sharkskin suit. The next night, we ate at the red-hot Pacific Time restaurant, located on a resurgent Lincoln Road Mall. At the next table over sat Cher, who looked like a *kabuki*, porcelain doll version of herself.

A couple of days later, fifteen of us rang in the New Year at Salvation. We ordered champagne. I lay on the floor and took a picture of everyone from below holding their flutes together, a disco ball center frame. After Salvation, with Trevor resting his chin on my shoulder like a slumbering dog, we cabbed it over to Hombre, "the club of last resort," as Hector referred to it. Hombre was a tiny hole in the wall with fog blown in so thick on the dance floor you couldn't see a thing, which revealed itself to be a blessing. There were drag queens, muscle boys, trannies, gangbangers, club kids, strippers, and one hulking bald guy who looked as though he'd just been banned from the set of an Ed Wood movie.

The next morning, Rachael and I did the vampire-walk back to the hotel, bathed in tropical sunshine. We were *so* last night. She wore a little dominatrix number, complete with black boots, short leather skirt, and fishnets. I had dropped my shirt in the bathroom at Hombre, took a look at the condition of the floor, and decided to let it rest in peace. I was down to my distressed leather pants and my shades: ostrich-skin framed sunglasses that strapped around my head and attached with Velcro. We traipsed right through the hotel lobby to the lounge where they served continental breakfast each morning. "After all, it's included," Rachael pointed out. We sat down to pick at bran muffins, sip orange juice and watch Oprah on TV, right next to a family of four from Brazil who did their best not to notice.

Next up was Mykonos for the Twelve Gods Party. I showed off by ordering from the *taverna* menus in Greek. The party was held under a spray of stars at the new Hard Rock Cafe, cut into the side of a craggy hill. We spent our days high on X at Go-Go Bar, an open-air lounge and pool set on the edge of a precipitous cliff overlooking Super Paradise Beach—as if ordinary paradise wouldn't do.

Afterwards, Rachael, Wes (and his red, spiked hair), Trevor and I went on to Istanbul to see a friend who had a prominent position at the American consulate. We got the tour of gay Istanbul, still very much on the downlow. There were lots of straight guys tired of chasing virtuous Turkish women, cruising dark little subterranean clubs for dick and rent boys. Turkish culture, it turned out, was rather tortured in its attitudes towards sexuality. Though men often turned to other men for sex, to label someone gay was an enormous insult, one that could easily get you knifed. With that in mind, we tried our best to ignore the male Turkish soldiers, who often strolled, armed and arm-in-arm, as if they were out on patrol with their high school sweethearts.

The following New Year's Eve, Hector, celebrating his six-figure contract to join a group of upscale boutique AIDS clinics, invited us to Rio de Janeiro. We dressed in white and joined the two million others gathered on the edge of Ipanema Beach. We enjoyed displays of fireworks and black magic courtesy of the *macumba* witch doctors, who spun and danced and chanted, which turned out to be a harbinger of what the three of us would do later, packed into a stifling Rio dance club.

In the evenings, Hector made a habit of disappearing for hours, often not returning to our hotel until the wee hours. He claimed he was out jogging. Back in New York, his latest boyfriend figured otherwise. They argued on the phone incessantly. By now, Hector was doing a ton of crystal, excessive even by the excessive standards of our group. But Hector was blessed with the constitution of a pack mule. He could stay up for days, grab a few hours' sleep and appear rested and composed. Maybe the rigors of medical school had prepared him for a life of drug abuse. Still, Rio was infamous for combining its easy attitudes regarding sex with easy access to the same. The incidence of AIDS here was on the rise, and I had to wonder if Hector, the famous AIDS researcher, might be as reckless as he was indiscreet.

The following summer, Trevor and Wes invited Rachael and me to their house in Provincetown, a sliver of sand and dunes at the very tip of Cape Cod, for many decades an artist community and gay mecca. Immediately, we connected with the place—its natural beauty, the lack of pretense, the way everyone blended.

One night, a hundred and fifty of us went out on a Fourth of July disco cruise aboard a whale watch boat. Christmas lights were strung along the deck, the Milky Way sparkled overhead, music thumped, flags snapped in the wind, boys perched, posed, and danced everywhere. I spent half the night sandwiched between Rachael and a friendly blonde lesbian from Boston who kept pressing a bumper of K into my hand, the other half sitting on deck, watching the sky go from indigo to amber to vermillion. When the sun broke the horizon, the deejay played "Here Comes the Sun" and I burst into tears.

Back at home, we began hosting dinner parties, cocktail parties—parties of all sort, the biggest of which was held on Rachael's thirty-sixth birthday, the day before Halloween. Rachael, Trevor, and I dressed as the three Lizas, circa *Cabaret*, complete with page-boy wigs and matching flapper dresses. Only Rachael shaved her legs. One couple came as Cruella de Vil and a Dalmatian. They had a three-way with another guest in our shower.

The next day, it took me hours and a whole can of turpentine to clean the theatrical grease paint off the tiles.

Jenny, a lesbian with a remarkable resemblance to the actress Sean Young, sat on my lap most of the night, until she drank too much and passed out in the living room. A very muscular man I'd never met before helped me carry her up three flights of stairs and put her into our bathtub. We removed her wine-stained shirt, and, while he held her hand, waited until she revived enough to call her girlfriend, who bore a remarkable resemblance to Ernest Borgnine. We carried Jenny, shirtless, back down the steps, through the crowded party, out the front door, across the street and into Jenny's car.

I can't even imagine what our neighbors, comprised of a government attorney, a professor, and their families, must have made of us. There just wasn't enough time or energy to make a big effort with them or anything else, including my music. I started bowing out of gigs, stopped practicing and eventually told the guys to find another drummer. I mean, how could being an anonymous drummer in a lame wedding band compare to being known world-wide as half of the straight couple who parties with the boys? Our pictures cropped up in gay magazines and websites, not to mention conversations. More than once, in locales as far-flung as Amsterdam, Sydney, and London, men who'd never met each other before found they had "Rachael and Nick" in common. We had become an entire subculture's six degrees of separation.

It wasn't all disco balls and fetish halls. There was, in fact, a life wedged in between the lifestyle, one that contained its own routines, pleasures, and drudgeries. Our house was nearly a hundred years old, and like any old home, required constant attention. There were projects: I scraped off the old paint from around the windowsills and refinished them. Rachael and I replanted the garden out front with a mix of blooming perennials and annuals. We had the wooden floors in the living room and dining room refinished, and, eventually, gave the kitchen a makeover consisting of fresh paint and new appliances.

As far as the day-to-day chores, most of them fell to me. I had always been fastidious regarding housecleaning, and now, with a much larger house to clean, I found myself dusting, spraying, vacuuming, and polishing something pretty much all the time. There was something about a clean house that gave me a tremendous sense of satisfaction, right down to the swoopy patterns left by the vacuum on the carpeting. Rachael wasn't a slob, but she was messy. I seemed to be always picking up after her. I hated the idea of an empty pantry and refrigerator, too, so, for the most part, I did all the shopping. And, the laundry, too. My efforts didn't go unacknowledged. In fact, Rachael would often see me coming in loaded down with groceries or outside, sweeping the back patio, and shake her head. "You do everything for me," she would say.

That wasn't entirely true. Rachael and her mother weren't close, but Rachael had managed to pick up some of her Spanish cooking skills and put them to use in our kitchen. She could knock out a fine paella and Spanish tortilla when she wanted to. Rachael also had a good eye for decoration, able to see a room and know just what it needed. Of course, if she needed advice all she had to do was ask one of our friends, many of whom lived in homes that looked like the cover of architectural design magazines.

One weekend, Wes came over and showed us how to mark off and measure the walls of the dining room to paint them contrasting vertical stripes. It was a tedious job that took us three times as long as we had planned, but we got it done. We found a large, dark wooden formal dining room table on sale at a local department store. Then, Rachael found uncovered slip chairs in a catalog and arranged for them to be recovered by the fellow who did upholstery for Wes. Rachael chose a green-gold iridescent fabric that seemed to glow. In the alley way, I found a pair of discarded authentic deco-era club chairs. They were in rough shape, but the bones were all there. Off they went to be reupholstered. And when the job was done, I stood back with my arms folded like a proud father, shaking my head in wonder at their magnificence. At a local antique store, Rachael found a lovely old wrought-iron chandelier, which I cleaned up and used to replace the existing ceiling fan. When everything was done, our dining room had become the heart of our house. With a fire crackling in the fireplace, the nice china out, and friends gathered around the table, we had achieved something I had never dreamed—a sense of permanence and of place. I was home.

Rachael was part of that home. Yes, she still had her tendency to be dramatic and controlling, but we seemed so thoroughly integrated into each other's lives. I could not imagine myself without her. And I was grateful, too. She had shown me a path to a life I was sure I could not have achieved on my own. Did gratitude constitute love? I thought so. Was there a price to be paid for love? As far as I could tell, always. My grandmother's love had come at the price of perpetual acquiescence. She had, as Rachael was doing now, run the show. Play the game their way, however, and the benefits were immediate and substantial.

As proof, all I needed to do was ask myself the same question Ronald Reagan had posed to the nation in his 1980 presidential campaign: Was I better off now than I had been four years earlier? I had substituted a life filled with self-doubt for one brimming with confidence, of self-pity and meagerness for self-indulgence and plenty, of isolation for inclusion, of denial for decadence, and of anonymity for a kind of celebrity. For the first time in my life, I felt as if I belonged. But I could not have answered the obvious follow-up question: belonged to what? This was not a lifestyle that was conducive to introspection. Had I spent more time thinking about my life, rather than burning through it, I might have realized that I didn't have a clue where things were headed, or about what might, or more importantly, should, come next.

At the time, none of that mattered. All I knew was that, against the Busby Berkeley spectacle of my life with Rachael and the circuit, presented in its wide-screen, Technicolor, Panavision, Smell-O-Rama, Cinerama, mama-jama, 3-D, Glow-in-the Dark, multi-story IMAX format, the rest of my life had been about as engaging as a faded black-and-white snapshot.

17

Enough

One chilly, clear night in early spring, Rachael and I sat in the Jacuzzi just outside the kitchen door, steam rising, her head leaning back against my arm.

"Feels good to do nothing," I said.

"Your birthday is coming up soon. Have you thought about what you want?"

"Want?"

"I was thinking a party in New York. Happens to be Gay Pride weekend."

"Aha."

"Hector would host it at his place in the city. Would you like that? A big party?"

"Sure," I said. "That would be great."

She paused a moment. "Are we doing okay?"

"I think we passed okay about five years ago."

"So, everything's good?"

The obvious answer to her question was hell yes. By any measurable standard, we had a wonderful life. Like Rachael always said, *more is more.* But was more enough? In quiet moments such as these, I had the sense that there was a flaw in the architecture of our life, a stress fracture deep in the foundation. Instead of tending to it, we just kept adding on new stories. Given just the right circumstances, would it collapse? The key was to avoid those circumstances.

"What are you worried about?" I asked.

"Everything. I'm a worrier."

"I noticed. Try to relax. Like this, see?" I sank a little deeper in the tub. "All of this. It's because of you. You know that, right?"

"You've worked hard."

"Sure. But I couldn't have done this myself. I wouldn't have believed it was possible."

"My job is to stop worrying. Yours is to start believing. So you feel good?"

"Why do you keep asking?"

Rachael looked away, dissatisfied. "Can't tell sometimes. You don't show much, either way."

"What is the problem?"

"This party. You don't seem very excited about it."

"That's not true. Who wouldn't want to celebrate their fortieth birthday at some fabulous place in Manhattan? What do you want me to do, cartwheels?"

"Once upon a time you would have. These days you seem so, I don't know. Flat."

Attenuated, was more like it. I was like a rhythm section, capable of blowing the doors off the joint, choosing, instead, to play in a whisper. Perhaps my tendency towards reserve was in direct response to Rachael's disinclination to exhibit the slightest bit of it. I had always admired people who could just put it out there to the world—people who didn't edit themselves. But that admiration also contained an element of fear. Could the quiet, sensitive boy ever stand up to someone like that?

"You're not the first to bring this up," I said.

"Though you may be the first to do so soaking naked in a hot tub."

"See, there you go," she said, stiffening, sending a shock wave of steamy water over the lip of the tub. "When the conversation gets too close, you get slippery."

"Sorry. It's an old trick I picked up along the way. When things get hot, you hide behind anything you can find—a table, a sofa, even a joke." I dipped my head beneath the water and resurfaced. "You're pretty good at it too, you know."

"You're right. I do that. But not with you. Besides, you're not a kid anymore." Rachael shook her head. "That grandmother of yours. Wish I had met her."

"That makes one of us."

"At least she didn't hit you."

"Sometimes I wish she had. I could have just hated her, nice and simple."

"There's nothing nice and simple about that. It's bad enough when you see it coming. You hear the footsteps coming up the stairs. The way the buckle on that belt used to jingle. It's bad, but you're ready for it. It's worse when you're just standing there and, for no reason you can figure, you get nailed. Nice and simple? Just ask my sisters: the hippy environmentalist, the schoolteacher wound up so tight she might implode, and the crazy bird lady that lives down the hall. Four sisters, right? Not one of us has children. What's the likelihood of that?"

"It's improbable."

"That's why it drives me crazy when you tell me how nice my parents are. Mr. and Mrs. Hit Now and Ask Questions Later."

"Have you noticed that the only problems we have regarding your parents is when I say something nice about them? Maybe they've changed. Maybe watching their children grow has healed whatever it was in them that made them so angry. That can happen. Or so I understand."

Rachael looked as though she had just confirmed an old suspicion. "So that's what this is about."

"Huh?"

"That's what's going on here. Just come out and say it. You wish you were with a woman who wasn't so messed up. Someone who would give you children."

"I thought what's going on here is that we were soaking in the hot tub."

"Admit it. You want kids."

I was always ambivalent about children. I hadn't witnessed a lot of good, stable parenting. And with Rachael being adamant about not having them, I'd put them out of my mind. "We talked about this a long time ago," I said. "Between your childhood and mine, it's better not to go there."

"People change. You just said so."

"People maybe. Not us."

"What's that supposed to mean?"

"It means, who says that a change would be for the better?" I put my arm around her. "Why risk what we have now? Besides, you're the one who always says the kid would be born with disco balls for eyes."

Rachael frowned. "It's okay to want things, to love things, to hate things, to get angry."

"I know."

"When we're with friends, you don't say much. Why is that?"

"You do a pretty good job for both of us."

"That's the only reason?"

"I prefer to observe."

"So tell me, Mr. Emotional Peeping Tom, what are you feeling right this moment?"

The image that came to mind was standing with my parents and a bunch of their musician friends staring at me, trying to get me to sing. As a kid, no one could make me sing. It was more than shyness. It was the reason I was guarded regarding all my emotions. The fear that if I tore open the packaging, the contents might spill out, and keep on spilling.

A few seconds passed. "Never mind," she said. "You'd think I asked you to saw off an arm."

Pretty close.

She said, "Maybe I'm just used to gay men. Most of them wear their emotions on their sleeve. Or, if they're your mom's friends, their poufy blouses." She reached over and tugged my earlobe. "So, now what?"

"What do you mean?" I said, defensive.

"I mean, I wonder what's next."

"Oh. Hell," I said, "I never expected *this*, much less a *next*. Can't this be enough?"

"Hmm." The edges of her mouth turned down. "Never thought of that."

Rachael and I took deep breaths, slipped down into water up to our chins and stared up at the sky.

18

A t the time, I thought our conversation in the hot tub was simply Rachael's call for reassurance. Looking back, I see it differently, as a plea—for me to take charge—to tell her there were going to have to be some changes in our life. We weren't kids anymore. It was time to start thinking about pulling out of the passing lane. We needed to, as W.C. Fields put it, "Take the bull by the tail and face the situation."

Of course, taking charge would have required me to visit a strange, parallel universe in which men told women what to do. Besides, our lifestyle wasn't particularly conducive to protracted periods of introspection.

Instead, we packed up whatever misgivings we might have had about the future and headed off to Oz. We arranged to stay at the studio of Rachael's friend, Sabrina, while she was away on a sales trip to Brazil. On our first night there, we decided to take it easy and rest up for what would be a full weekend of festivities. Instead, we invited Trevor and Wes over to try a dose of mushrooms. My previous experience with mushrooms had been light and enjoyable, like a mild, three-hour hit of laughing gas, minus the oral surgery.

We boiled the mushrooms into a tea the color (and aroma) of dirty dish water and sipped it down. Pharmacologically speaking, the evening was a bust. Rachael threw up, then fell asleep with her head in my lap. Trevor and Wes felt nothing and left early.

There I sat, slumped on Sabrina's futon, enjoying the quiet as I stroked Rachael's head while she slept. At the time, Sabrina was going through her I'm-edgy-so-I-wear-only-black phase. The statement was also reflected in her design choices. Her studio was well appointed but decorated in a rather limited palette that ranged all the way from dusky gray to midnight black. I was just about to gently lift Rachael's head off my lap and get ready for bed, when I noticed, set directly in front of me on the lacquered dresser, a black-and-white portrait of Sabrina mounted in a brushed-silver frame.

Sabrina, smiling slyly and looking as lovely as always, gazed back at me. Then, ever so slowly, her smile drooped to a frown, as if a voice I couldn't hear was whispering in Sabrina's ear the saddest story ever told. Her eyes welled with tears. I watched, mesmerized, as the portrait was transformed into a lament. Tears streamed down her cheeks, collected at the bottom edge of the photo, and flowed down the frame. What was this? A message? An omen? I forced myself to look away, hoping the vision could be erased. But when I looked back, Sabrina was just as I had left her, grief stricken and mournful.

I sat there staring at the portrait a long time, waiting to see what would happen next. Nothing did. Finally, I drifted off into a restless sleep filled with dreams I would never remember.

Sky High

My birthday party and my state of mind were the same. Fifty-four floors high to be exact, in Hector's new apartment with floor to ceiling windows and the Empire State Building framed dead center. The crowd swirled, glasses clinked, bleached teeth flashed. The groove was definitely on.

I stood in the kitchen staring slack-jawed at the blender. It was all Wes's fault, God love him. Thirty hits of X in one blender full of cranberry juice. That was his birthday gift to me. Broken capsules and empty Dixie cups were strewn across the olive-colored granite countertop. Thirty hits in one blender. I was too high to do the math.

The music pulsed through me, waves of it, like a heartbeat. Such a party. I should have been out there mingling, like Rachael, but not just yet. I needed to hold on to something. I decided on the granite countertop, smooth and cool and solid.

Here was Wes, his pupils the size of manhole covers, "Doing okay?" He put his arm on my shoulder.

"Only the best day of my life." I leaned on Wes, lovely Wes. No words could describe how much I loved him. "Thank you, my friend."

"My pleasure, honey. Actually, your pleasure, by the looks of you."

The music changed to "You're Free," Ultra Nate's anthem *du jour*, on every circuit deejay's play list, bursting forth from a thousand boom boxes on Fire Island, Rehoboth, and Provincetown. I hated screaming diva anthems, but right then, it was working for me. Working just fine.

Wes said, "Listen, Nicky, are you going to be here for a while?"

I looked at Wes, trying to figure out where the hell I would go. He patted my face. "I'll take that as a yes. Be right back. We got you something special."

Before I could thank him, he was gone.

One thing was for sure, that vision I had at Sabrina's and that weird run-in with Bianca, the clairvoyant drag queen, seemed like a million years ago. I should have invited Bianca here, shown *her* who belonged and who didn't.

Someone tapped me on the shoulder.

I turned and there was Trudie, sitting on the other end of the countertop, her legs dangling down from a sundress as thin as rice paper. She had come up on the train from Baltimore. I hadn't seen her since that night at our house. She was tan. Looking good. She smiled at me, showing off those dimples. I never knew how much I had a thing for dimples. I slid down the counter towards her, tapping on the marble with my fingertips like I was playing a piano, right up and over her thighs. She spread her knees so I could rest in between them. Sweet. A cloud of velvet shrouded us.

"You tried the punch." I said.

"It's that obvious?" She touched her flushed cheeks with the tips of her fingers.

"You look about how I feel."

Her eyes drifted down. "You look like you feel pretty good."

"Good line."

"Having a nice birthday?"

"Uh, huh."

"Going out later?"

"I expect."

"Good. So do I."

Two in a row. I gave her a kiss. Not too long or too hard. I tried to end it, but her legs scissored behind me as her mouth pressed against mine, her tongue between my lips. She dropped her legs and it was over. For now. I *ruled*. I was *the man* in a tight, black Versace shirt and Diesel jeans.

Here were Wes, Hector, and Rachael, smirking, like they were in on the same secret.

Rachael put my hands on her cheeks. "I could power the entire Eastern Seaboard." She dragged her thumb across my lips. "What's up with the lipstick? Are we entering a new phase?"

I considered making up an excuse. Why bother? "Some birthday wishes from Trudie."

Rachael smiled. "It's not your shade." She kissed me. I thought about Trudie.

"Okay, lovebirds," Wes said. "How about a little decorum." Wes was hiding something behind his back. "We got you something." He held out a brass plaque.

"What's this?"

"Read it."

My eyes wouldn't focus. I held it away at arm's length and covered one eye with my hand.

"Here, I'll do it," Rachael said.

> "In recognition of years of effort, by unanimous decision of fags everywhere, Nicholas Garnett shall, from this day forward, be honored as THE GAYEST STRAIGHT MAN IN AMERICA, with all accorded rights and privileges."

"I'm touched," I said. Everyone was smiling. "Where's Trevor?"

"He had two cups of the punch," Wes said. "He sends his best wishes."

Someone asked, "How about a speech?"

The room was packed with people, many of whom I didn't even know. I should have been nervous, but just then I could have addressed a joint session at the United Nations.

"Help me up," I said.

"Up where?" Rachael asked.

"The counter."

"You're going to stand on the counter and give a speech?" Rachael asked. "Who are you and what have you done with my husband?"

Their hands were all over me, lifting, pushing, and before I knew it, I was standing on the kitchen counter, holding the plaque. Heads turned, fingers tapped on shoulders and pointed to me. My nerves cracked. What was I thinking? I turned around to get down, but they were standing behind me, shaking their heads *no*, pushing me back and snickering like kids. Someone turned the music down.

Across the room, there stood Trevor. It was hard to miss him, wearing a sparkly silver shirt, shoulders pressed against the glass as if he was hanging on meat hooks. He didn't seem at all surprised to see me standing there on the kitchen counter holding a plaque. He gave me big thumbs up. There was a *real* friend for you.

"Um, hi there." I waved. Everyone quieted down. My forehead and armpits turned prickly hot from flop sweat. I froze. I needed to think of something, anything, to say. I took a deep breath. Adrenaline worked its magic. My heart pounded and I felt sharp and clear.

"I know this may be hard to believe, but there was a time I could be seen out in public wearing pleated khakis. My apartment looked like a Salvation Army warehouse. I said 'hey, man' and 'dude.' I was headed towards a future of boys-night-outs at the local sports bar, a couple of kids, and Costco." I held up my index finger. "Not that there's anything wrong with that." Everyone laughed. "That's all changed. You should see me fluff our house for a dinner party. I can quote several lines of dialogue from *The Women*, and I know what a peplum is. I know there are plenty of people that think my life is bizarre. But look around. Is there anywhere else you'd want to be today?"

Everyone yelled, "No!"

"My wife and friends have presented me with this plaque proclaiming me the gayest straight man in America." I held it above my head. "I'll do my best to live up to that honor." There was thunderous applause. I bowed. Hands helped me down, and I was showered with hugs, gropes, and kisses. High as a kite, on top of the world.

20

Highway from Hell

"*P*lease slow down, Nick," Rachael said from the back seat.

"Relax," I said. "This car is made to go fast."

"Not at night and not in the rain. And not after you've been up partying for a day and a half."

"How about you go back to your conversation and let me drive."

"I'd be happy to. After you slow the fuck down."

I grunted and let off the accelerator, just a little.

We were somewhere on the Jersey Turnpike. Cranky, cracked out, and exhausted. It was me and Rachael, Trevor, and Wes, on the highway from hell, headed back to D.C. from my birthday party. The mood was distinctly not pretty. The four of us couldn't have mustered enough serotonin to cheer up an amoeba.

"Sorry," Rachael said, "I'm just trying to get us home alive."

"So we can get suicidal in the comfort of our own home?" I said.

"No one made you get up at eight in the morning and party all day."

"You're going to lecture me? Did I shove crystal up your nose?"

"Did I do it all goddamn day long?"

"Actually, you did."

"*Now, now,* kids," Trevor said, slumped against the passenger door, his leather jacket draped over him like a blanket. "Why don't we let Wes continue with his story?"

"Sorry," Rachael said. "Of course. Please go on."

Wes had been recounting the story of the breakup of his marriage and how he'd come out to his wife. Very poignant. Given my state of mind, overly so.

"Remind me. Where was I?" Wes asked. He was in the rear seat, leaning against the door, his head resting on a pillow.

"You and Marsha were high school sweethearts," Rachael said.

"Right. Sounds corny, but we really were. The all-American couple. We did the usual teenage stuff together. Rock concerts. Keg parties. Even went through a Goth phase. Believe it or not, Trevor, I spent my junior year of high school wearing black eyeliner and hair halfway down my back."

"That explains so much," Trevor said.

"Anyway, after we graduated, we moved in together. I got a job as a security guard at the mall, started night school, and she became a secretary at a law firm. We got married a year later, bought a little house, got a dog, thought we'd be together forever."

"And you had no idea?" Rachael asked.

"I wouldn't admit it, not even to myself. Not for years."

"Years?" I said.

"Sounds crazy. Even to me. Eventually, I couldn't ignore it anymore. I finally got up the nerve to go to a gay bar one night. Soon as I walked through those doors, I knew."

"And Marsha, she never suspected?" Rachael said. "Thought I might be messing with other women. But I made a promise I'd never cheat on her."

My stomach tightened.

Rachael said, "Not once?"

"I couldn't have lived with myself."

I felt queasy.

"I was so unhappy. So was she. I just couldn't bring myself to tell her. Then one night she sits me down. Asks me if I'm having an affair."

Rachael blew her nose. "And?"

"I had to tell her. It's the hardest thing I'll ever have to do. At least I hope it is. I moved out the next day."

"How'd she take it?" I asked.

"Wouldn't believe me at first. Then she got furious. Everything you'd expect."

My hands gripped the steering wheel so hard I might have snapped it in two.

"So brave," Rachael said. "But you must have been relieved, too? At least you could finally start living your life."

"Not until we were divorced."

My mouth was so dry I could barely speak. "You didn't have sex with a man until your divorce was final?"

"I think it's the reason we're such good friends now. She's thanked me a million times for waiting."

Rachael gasped. "That is the saddest, most beautiful story I've ever heard."

Wes pulled Rachael closer. Her body heaved. "I think we're all a little tender right about now. How about a lovely Ambien to take the edge off?"

"Good idea," I said. Wes rummaged through his jacket. He pulled out a pill bottle and shook one out onto Rachael's palm.

She swallowed the pill. "I don't know how you did it."

Neither did I. I glanced at Wes in the rear view mirror, feeling equal parts admiration and resentment. Could I do what Wes had done? Allow love to trump desire? Based on recent events, the answer was a resounding no. God, I wished that I was gay and all I had to do was admit I had finally given in to it. No, my dirty little secret couldn't be explained away by sublimated sexuality. I was a straight guy, all right. The worst kind.

After my award acceptance speech, I had gone to the bathroom, and Trudie was coming out. I blocked her at the entrance. We didn't say a word. We didn't have to. She took me by the hand, we crossed the hall into the bedroom and locked the door behind us.

That morning I couldn't get Rachael out of bed, so I went to Twilo by myself. Twilo, a subterranean mosh-pit, was still raging from the night before. Trudie was there. I knew she would be. We went back to her hotel room for crazy-ass-porn-bust-up-the-furniture sex—the kind Rachael and I didn't have. I got back to Hector's just in time to take a shower and pack.

The bedroom incident at Trevor's I could explain away, at least to myself. I was high and pumped up from the party. Rachael wouldn't like it, but she might understand. But what happened that morning? That was different. Premeditated. Unforgivable. Worst of all, I liked it. I liked it a lot. Even then, through the guilt and shame and fear I felt a spike of excitement. I shivered and broke into a guilt-infused sweat. I hated myself. I wanted more.

"You okay?" Trevor looked at me from the passenger seat. Car headlights played across his face like searchlights.

"Just tired."

"Want me to drive?"

"No. It's not much farther."

"That was some epic birthday. We'll be talking about it until you're eighty."

In the rearview mirror, I saw Rachael, sound asleep, leaning against Wes's shoulder, his arm draped across her. Trevor peeked over the headrest into the back seat.

"Sleeping angels."

I kept my eyes on the road.

"Are things okay with you and Rachael?"

"Why do you ask?"

"Things seem tense."

"Everything's fine."

Trevor sighed. "Glad to hear it. Lord knows, after fifteen years, Wes and I have had our share of everything. Including tense."

I glanced over at him. "How do you deal?"

"Talk it out. Sometimes you wait it out. One thing's for sure, it's time to park the party bus for a while." He rubbed his eyes. "I'm going to close my eyes for a few minutes, okay?"

"Sure thing."

Trevor shifted around, settling in.

The rain had let up. I punched the accelerator and the engine kicked down into overdrive. We surged ahead with a force that shocked me, just before it made me smile.

21

Heavenly Bodies

I returned home from my birthday party certain of two things: Rachael could never know about what happened with Trudie, and it could never happen again. I had no doubt of the outcome if I gave in to the temptation. Even *no limits* had its limits. And those limits were catching up to me. I had to stay away from Trudie, keep myself distracted, or risk everything.

Fortunately, the circuit was nothing if not distracting. By then, even conservative, staid Washington, D.C. had tossed its glow stick into the circuit mix with the unfortunately named event, Cherries Jubilee. Ridiculous name notwithstanding, having a circuit event in our backyard felt like the circus had come to town. We made arrangements with Anna and the staff to hold down the fort at Big Bark and plunged right in.

One afternoon at an outdoor block party, we were introduced by Hector to Jason, a personal trainer. Jason was a gravelly-voiced, two-hundred-and-twenty pounds of beef on the hoof, with an IQ slightly north of his body fat percentage, which was an assessment based more on my ego than the limits of his intellect. Anyone who looked like him deserved to be dumb. To my astonishment and Rachael's delight, Jason was also straight. I was surprised. Rachael was infatuated.

Another straight guy in this scene? My surprise was quickly overcome by a stab of an emotion I didn't expect: jealousy. Not from Rachael's fawning. It was the interest he was generating from the other boys. I'd never had to share the spotlight with another straight guy, and although I pretended to be indifferent to the attention, a part of me liked it, more than I would admit.

That night, we went to TRAX with Jason and Mandy, his trainer girlfriend who had a face like Minnie Driver and a voice like Minnie Mouse. Though Mandy had never been with another woman, she took quite a shine to Rachael, an attraction she made no effort to conceal, and one that led to an evening of Jason and me exchanging satisfied smiles as we watched Mandy and Rachael paw at each other for long stretches on the dance floor.

We closed TRAX. On the way out someone handed Jason a tiny slip of paper the size of a Chinese fortune with the address of an after-hours party. It took us an hour to find the cracked-out shell of a building, four floors above a palm reading business. We worked our way upstairs, stepping over chunks of cement and graffiti-covered plaster, paid ten dollars each to get into the decrepit two-bedroom flat some enterprising soul had converted into a disco, and danced until dawn.

With the sun peeking over the squalor of the neighborhood, the time came to seal the deal.

"So," said Rachael, "as creepy as this may sound, how about a nightcap in our hot tub?"

Mandy said, "Love to, but I have to go."

"Go?" I repeated.

"I have to meet my mother. It's her birthday. I promise though," Mandy said brightly, "we'll get together soon. For sure."

As Jason walked Mandy out to get a cab, Rachael turned to me. "You're going to have to go with me on this one," Rachael said, nodding towards Jason, who was headed back our way.

In the cab ride over to Jason's apartment near Dupont Circle, I tried to block out the image of watching Conan the Barbarian have sex with my wife. There was one thought I couldn't shake, though. What if Jason wasn't as straight as he let on? He certainly talked a good game. Rachael had asked him how he felt being constantly surrounded by gay men.

"That's my clientele. If the boys want to pay me $150 an hour to train them and I have to get a little flirty, that's all right by me. If I was gay, I'd be just another $50 an hour fag trainer."

One look at Jason's apartment, however, quelled my doubts. The dirty dishes in the sink, the mauve Herculon sofa, the harsh lighting, the bad art hung way too high, and the clincher—the complete boxed set of *Van Halen*. By comparison, my little bachelor pad had been Liberace's boudoir.

"I don't mind telling you guys, I am tweaked," Jason said, as he reached down to take the vial and rolled-up bill from Rachael. "I usually stick to cocaine. This stuff gets a bit intense."

As I watched Jason prance around his living room,

I felt my energy and my libido sag. I looked over at Rachael, glassy eyed and drawn. Just under the thin crust of our high, our bodies were screaming for food and rest, our serotonin-depleted brains furious at us, no doubt planning their revenge. We should have been in bed hours ago. Sitting in Jason's shabby apartment in my sweaty club clothes with grimy gray light coming through his crooked venetian blinds, I felt *very* last night—verging on last month. We had pushed it, right to the limit and past.

"Guess I'd better do some of that too," I said.

Rachael handed me the vial. Jason sat next to Rachael on the sofa and she looked over at me, smiled, and patted the cushion on the other side. I slid over.

"How are you feeling?" she asked me.

"A little weird."

"Same here," said Jason.

Rachael rubbed our thighs. "Just let me handle things."

The crystal rallied me for one last surge. It was now or never, I thought, as I unbuttoned my jeans.

22

Prelude to a Kiss

Thursday nights at Trevor and Wes's had become a tradition destined to become a legend. As Wes's customer base had grown, so had the demands placed on his time and his relationship. Much to Trevor's dismay, customers began to call and show up at their door at all hours of the day and night. At Trevor's urging, Wes announced that henceforth, business would only be conducted on Thursday nights between the hours of eight and eleven p.m., when Trevor would be out of the house working at his restaurant. Surprisingly, with the exception of an occasional four a.m. call of desperation, everyone had complied.

Ever the gracious host, Wes had infused Thursday evenings with some of his Savannah-bred southern hospitality. Folks dropped by for a leisurely chat and a cocktail as they stocked up for the weekend. With Wes holding court behind his broad walnut custom made desk set in the corner of their tastefully decorated Sixteenth Street townhouse, Thursday nights felt much more like *Gone with the Wind* than crack den.

The clientele was nothing if not eclectic. It ranged from Van Chen, the frail, birdlike Vietnamese seamstress who had produced our window treatments, to Jay Silver, Rachael's dashing gynecologist with the movie-star looks.

One of the few reminders of the business at hand was the ever-present hangers-on, usually young, cute boys serving cocktails and making runs to the safe in the basement to bring up the raw materials. These items, Wes dispensed like a pharmacist. Every so often, a friend—Wes always referred to customers as "friends" even if he'd never laid eyes on them—would arrive in a hurry, but that was just tough luck for them. Wes expected a certain level of decorum. Friends could count on several minutes of polite banter before getting down to business, signaled by him asking in his lilting drawl, "And what can I do for you this evening, honey?"

One evening, Trevor came home early, took a look around his living room and tried to shake Wes out of his complacency, pointing out that the night had become so popular that "if the police ever raid this place, they'd be booking people as fast as the express check-out at Walmart on Christmas Eve."

By then, it was too late. The evening had insinuated itself into our hearts and minds, not to mention our calendars.

On this particular evening, Rachael, Trevor, and I sat on the sofa in Wes's living room, cocktails in hand, discussing our plans to invite Jason and Mandy to Fire Island for the Morning Party.

"So, I figure, what better place to initiate our newbies? Just imagine the four of us unleashed on Fire Island," Rachael said.

"Oh, I'm imagining it," Trevor said. He took a sip of his cocktail and shook his head.

"You mean that article?" Rachael asked. The previous Sunday, the *Times* had run an expose regarding the excesses of the circuit scene and how far it had strayed from its altruistic origins. Morning Party on Fire Island was singled out for its tolerance of rampant sex and blatant drug use.

"It has gone a bit over the top," Trevor said.

"Over the top?" Rachael said. "May I remind you all whose home we're sitting in? And what goes on here. "She glanced over to the coffee table on which there was set a round mirror, the top of which was partially obscured by white powder. "By the way, Wes, what is this?"

Wes glanced up from his desk. "Help yourself."

"Cocaine," Rachael said, sounding as though someone showed her a photo of a puppy. "*So* four years ago." She licked her finger, dipped it in the powder and rubbed it on her gums.

"Look," Trevor said, "I'm going to assume I can't talk you out of anything, but at least let me be able to say I warned you. Fire Island is not conducive to relationships. I can't tell you how many couples I've seen come out of that place totally fucked. Messing around with another couple is new to you guys. The four of you hardly know each other."

"I expect we'll know each other a bit better after a few days," I said, then winked at Rachael.

"I always said," added Rachael, "the next best thing to having a successful relationship is ruining one."

Trevor winced. "*Lovely.* All I'm saying is this isn't like that thing with Trudie, a one-night hook-up."

I crossed and uncrossed my legs.

"You're going to be together for days in a pressure cooker, with Hector in charge of the stove. That alone should scare the hell out of you."

Someone knocked at the door, and I went over and opened it. It was that lobbyist whose name I couldn't ever remember. He looked past me to Wes, whose etiquette demanded an invitation before entering. From across the room, Wes said, "Rob, darling. Be right with you." Rob entered. I swung the door shut behind him, walked back over, and sat on the arm of the sofa.

I said to Trevor, "We're not exactly neophytes."

"Yes, but this time you're throwing sex in the mix," said Trevor. "Keep your emotions out of it. Think of it as an Olympic event."

"Sport fucking," Rachael said.

"Exactly," Trevor said.

A young boy in a tight white tank top came over. "Anyone up for another drink?" he asked.

"I'll take a refresh on this," Trevor said. He handed him his glass. Trevor eyed him up and down as he walked away.

Using my toe, I tapped Trevor on his shin. "You were saying?"

"Right. Now, it's true, foursomes are the best formula because no one feels left out, but that only works if you all stay together. And you're going to be tempted not to, trust me. Another thing. Pace yourselves. And watch the G," Trevor added. "Especially the G."

Rachael threw up her hands. "You're preaching to the choir. Stuff makes me queasy." She motioned to me. "It's this one you need to talk to."

GhB had spread quickly through the scene. It was cheap, easy to carry and consume (just pour a little vial full in a bottle of Gatorade), and it gave you a warm, fabulous high, similar to ecstasy but without the hangover or depression. Unfortunately, the same dose which delivered that delicious buzz the last twenty times, could, the very next time, throw you into a coma, suppress your respiratory system and kill you.

Usually, it was Rachael under the spotlight for her drug use. I didn't like being the center of this kind of attention. "Got it," I said. "Anything else?" I asked.

Trevor nodded. "Matter of fact, there is. Don't wait until you're knee deep in cha-cha at the Pavillion to work this stuff out with them. Set some ground rules and talk about them *before* you get there. This is Fire Island, my pets. Morning Party. The big freaky-deaky."

"Damn," Rachael said. "Should I be writing all this down?"

Trevor patted her cheek. "Laugh now, but you're getting privileged information here, the result of years of fuck-ups. Wes, what do you think?" he yelled.

Wes held a stack of money in one hand and several baggies in the other. His latest hairdo, shoulder-length dreadlocks, nearly obscured his face. "About what, darling?"

"About our hetero couple here cavorting around Morning Party with a similarly inclined twosome, exchanging precious bodily fluids."

"What does the other couple look like?"

"It's those personal trainers," Rachael said.

"If you don't do them, I will."

Rachael said, "You can always count on Wes to see the big picture."

Trevor waved off Wes dismissively. He turned to us. "Look at that hair. Why would I ask *that one* anything involving responsible behavior?"

"Everything will be just fine," said Rachael. "Mandy's lovely and sincere, and Jason's cool."

"Maybe so, but here's one more thing you aren't going to want to hear. Even if you do everything I just told you to do, which you won't, you're still risking your marriage every time you mess around with other people."

"How do you guys still manage?" I asked. Of our many friends with non-exclusive relationships, Trevor and Wes seemed to be the best at avoiding the emotional minefields, employing a policy of full participation when they were together and discretion when they weren't, an arrangement I referred to as "Don't ask, don't smell."

"It is different with boys. We've got a knack separating our heads from our dicks. Even so, you never know when you'll stick your willy somewhere and the damn thing blows up like an exploding cigar."

"Nice," I said, clutching my crotch.

"Then come with us," Rachael said. "Save us from our baser instincts."

"Spend all of Morning Party trying to manage the four of you? Sounds fabulous. Wes and I had a hard enough time managing ourselves."

"Do tell," Rachael said.

"There was a certain party featuring a whip, a dildo and a piñata." Trevor pinched the bridge of his nose with his fingers as though he had suddenly been afflicted by a vicious headache. "Do I need to say more?"

23

Fairy Boats

Rachael, a dozen or so gay men, and I stood by Dr. Hector's poolside Jacuzzi on Fire Island and watched Jason and Mandy. Again. It was sex, but it wasn't particularly sexy—more *Animal Planet* than *Spice Channel*. Mandy had braced herself against the edge of the blue fiberglass tub, her ropy black hair spilling down in front of her except for the thick band Jason had gathered in both fists. With each of his thrusts, a swell of water cascaded over the lip of the tub to the deck below. The sound of water slapping wood blended with the couple's staccato rasps and grunts to form an oddly syncopated rhythm. It was a pretty slick groove, actually—somewhere between *bossa nova* and Barry White.

The faces on the men gathered around the couple were rapt. Who could blame them? This was at least as good as any porn movie, *and* it was the real thing, *and* it involved a hot straight man with huge muscles and tattoos.

I turned to Rachael and she gave me a different take—annoyance.

Trevor had been wrong about Fire Island. It was more. Much more. The place was as over the top as William Shatner reciting Shakespeare. Narrow boardwalks wound through pine forests and connected the houses together like the yellow brick road. Trees reverberated with the *clickity-clack* of big men pulling little red wagons full of groceries and luggage to and from the ferry terminal. There were miles of desolate sand dunes and achingly beautiful seagrass-lined beaches.

But all that bucolic splendor was just a set-up for what this place was really all about: bug-eyed excess, where a summer share set you back the cost of a three-bedroom rambler in Paducah; huge, lavish parties; smaller, yet more lavish parties; social climbing galore; one-upmanship; balls-to-the-wall, twenty-four, seven.

The only nightclub, the Pavilion, was a wooden sweat box. In the morning, a stream of tweaked-out zombies shuffled shamelessly along the walkways on the prowl for their house or an after party, but mostly for sex. On Monday mornings, the human effluence made its jittery, sleep-deprived way down to the dock for the bucket-of-blood ferry boat back to Sayville.

It wasn't easy to figure out appropriate standards of behavior, especially at Hector's house, a deceptively cozy, two-story wooden structure with an enormous deck overlooking Great South Bay. Hector was certainly a generous host. K, G, X, poppers, weed, Viagra, crystal—if it wasn't right there in front of you, all you had to do was ask. The only thing in short supply was food. One morning, I opened Hector's fridge to find nothing but a bag of frozen pierogies, which Hector, wearing a black leather thong, served up one afternoon by the pool—Fire Island's version of high tea. One evening, I watched Hector do fat rails of crystal and had to wonder how much longer he could keep it up. He was still managing his career, still pulling himself together during the week, "breaking the cycle" as he called it with massive doses of

Klonapin. But among our friends in New York, word was that he was slipping, that his colleagues and patients were noticing a change in him.

He seemed flightier than ever. The day before, he'd mentioned he was thinking about turning the grounds of the house into a shelter for abused animals.

"What a lovely idea," Rachael said. "What kind?"

"I was thinking giraffes."

The first people Hector introduced us to were the Porn Boys, featured acts in a popular series of gay videos. I kept forgetting their real names, which was awkward considering how often I ran into them traipsing around the house naked. The Porn Boys had a steady stream of visitors. The first time I walked by their room, I'd been frozen in place by the sight of a naked rugby scrum. Based on what I saw, it was a high-scoring game.

The Porn Boys made orgies look easy, so Rachael and I decided to give it a try with Jason and Mandy. We should have left the porn to the professionals. At first, the sex with Jason and Mandy had a dreamy quality, as if I were watching myself through a Vaseline-coated camera lens. Then, things got all too real. I happened upon Rachael and Jason having sex in the poolside shower. I pretended that it didn't bother me. But it did. That night, Mandy woke me up in the middle of the night to see the stars. We jumped in the pool and had sex as the sun came up. The next evening, Rachael and I walked into the guest bedroom and found Mandy pancaked between Jason and Hector's boyfriend. Hector played it off as though it didn't bother him, but Rachael was mortified that our guests had pilfered our host's date.

On Fire Island, a pair of attractive straight couples were as rare as a flock of albino ostriches. Word spread.

That's when Jason and Mandy began having sex-on-demand. And demand was strong. The previous night, we all went over to the neighbor's pool to watch the sunset. Rachael and I headed back to the house, leaving Jason and Mandy, who, at the urging of the crowd, had sex on a lounge chair. When they were done, we could hear the applause all the way from Hector's living room.

Rachael was jealous, but not of Mandy. Jason and Mandy had become the show. We were used to being *the* hot straight couple in this scene. After having the spotlight for so long, Rachael wasn't going to be satisfied with second billing.

Just as Trevor had predicted, Rachael and I pitched all his sage advice overboard the second we boarded the ferry. Right off the bat, I fell into a crush. With Mandy. It happened in the shallow end of the pool, her legs wrapped around my waist.

"You know, I think I'm a little ga-ga."

My heart raced. "That makes two of us," I said.

"It's not just his looks."

Oh. "I see," I said.

He's so good to me. A genuinely nice guy. Slide back a little." I did. She swiveled her hips and lowered herself onto me. Mandy, languid now, let her head lean to one side and closed her eyes.

"Does he know how you feel?"

"Oh, he knows, all right. But I just can't get him to make a commitment. At least not the way I want him to." Her thigh muscles pulsed against my hips. "I'd be monogamous in a heartbeat with him. And you and Rachael, of course. Pull my hair. Harder."

While having sex with an acquaintance, Mandy was proposing a monogamous relationship involving four people, two couples—one of them married—living in different cities, a union comprised of two heterosexual men and a couple of bisexual women.

I made one serious attempt to bond with Jason. He was, after all, the only other straight guy around for miles. One morning, during a rare quiet moment while Rachael and Mandy were in the shower, he and I sat at the edge of the pool in the shimmering sun, our feet dangling in the water.

"You know," I said, "the girls are probably having sex in there right now."

Jason looked back over his shoulder and shook his head. "I never thought I'd say this, but I don't care. It's been kind of nonstop."

"Yeah, I noticed." Jason didn't bite, so I moved on. "How are you and Mandy doing?"

"Hell if I know. Ah, she's okay. You know, all you have to do is pay some attention, tell them you love them every once in a while."

"Do you?"

"She's a sweet girl, and the sex is great, but," he shrugged, "not having to deal with women and their bullshit is one reason I hang with the boys. It's simpler. And more fun. I swear to God, I wish I was gay. With these dudes—" he spun his index finger in a circle—"it's one big party all the time. Fuck—" he slapped his palms together—"and move on. Which is the way it should be. Think about it. If it weren't for pussy, what good would women be?"

I stopped churning my feet. There it was: exactly the attitude Rachael claimed lurked just below the surface of most straight men, even easy-going Jason who'd just bared his inner misogynist.

"I tell you what," he continued, "the day someone builds a female robot with the right anatomy, one that'll fuck you and keep her mouth shut, on that day, my friend, women will be obsolete."

Elegant and terrifying logic. Strong women had been such a big part of my life. I had never even considered the possibility of a world in which they didn't exist.

Rachael and Mandy came out of the house together, fresh from the shower. Rachael had her towel tied just above her breasts, Mandy, just below. I was tempted to shatter Rachael and Mandy's illusion about Jason, that he was so cool and evolved and nice. But we were all skating on thin ice. Plus, there was Mandy to consider. Quite a lot of Mandy.

"What's going on here?" Rachael asked.

"Jason and I were just sharing a utopian dream of a world without chaos and drama and—"

"Let me guess," said Rachael. "Me?"

Jason and I laughed and stared at our feet.

24

G Forces

Back in the hot tub, Jason finally finished with Mandy. A couple of the men applauded. Polite, dry clapping. I leaned over to Rachael and said, "Maybe we should start charging admission." She glared at me.

Hector emerged from the house. "Guys, we really should head on over." Four men were crowded around the Jacuzzi, hovering around Jason and Mandy like the paparazzi at Cannes.

Rachael said, "This is getting ridiculous."

"I don't see how making a scene is going to help things."

"We did not invite them here just to humiliate us." She turned back towards Jason and Mandy, who by now had emerged from the Jacuzzi and were being toweled off by two very attentive men. "Don't worry. As usual, I'll handle it."

"What's really bothering you?" I asked. "The fact that it's Mandy in the Jacuzzi with Jason and not you?"

"You've got nerve. After those late-night stargazing sessions in the pool?"

"Why don't you go back inside and smoke some more crack. It brings out a lovely side of you."

Hector put his hands on our shoulders. "Shall we go?"

Rachael hooked her arm in his. "Yes. Let's."

Fifteen minutes later, Hector, Rachael, Jason, Mandy, and I waited to enter the oh-so-fabulous house party thrown by a New York power couple, rumored to be big-time meth dealers. They had clearly spared no expense, importing nightclub-quality sound and lights and hiring the red-hot deejay, Victor Calderone, turning their spacious bayside deck into *the* place to be. Hector had, once again, worked his magic connections and procured tickets, which was no small feat. Everyone had been talking about this party for days, cranking up the buzz to a deafening screech.

We got in a short line at the gated entrance to the property. On the other side of the tall redwood fence rumbled the telltale thump of music. The gate keepers consisted of a gigantic black bouncer, accompanied by a hostess. She was waif-like, with alabaster skin and a braided ponytail that reached far down her back. The hosts had left nothing to chance, which meant underneath that delicate exterior, there certainly lurked the soul of a cold, reptilian assassin, able to slice off your balls with one pass of those perfectly manicured nails.

She stood there holding her clipboard, flanked by the bouncer in his silly Hawaiian shirt (tonight's party theme was "jungle fever"), dealing with some unlucky boy wearing a palm-tree print sarong and black combat boots.

"Look, I'm sure I'm on the list," he said. He attempted to lean over the clipboard. "T-u-r-n-e-r," he spelled it out slowly.

I whispered to Mandy, "As if there are a million other ways to spell it."

She giggled and squeezed my arm.

"I'm sorry, no," said the Ice Princess. "I've checked twice." Her smile was perfect. And chilling.

"Can you call Bradley over? I'm sure he can straighten this out. We talked about it in Miami."

"I'm sorry, no. The hosts and I went over the guest list earlier just so I wouldn't have to bother him this evening."

Polite, sensible, consistent, and firm. A real pro. We could have used her at Big Bark.

"If you just let me in for one minute—"

"I'm sorry, no. I'm not allowed to let anyone in without a ticket."

"Well then, I'll buy a ticket." He reached down into his boot and removed a wad of bills.

"I'm sorry, no. All the tickets for the party have been sold."

"Oh, come *on*." His voice became a full falsetto. "Look, I don't care what it costs."

"This party is sold out. Unless you have a ticket, I'm afraid I can't help you." She looked past the boy, brightened, and smiled, revealing her astoundingly white teeth. "I didn't see you standing there."

Hector moved past the boy, who was busy snapping out several twenty-dollar bills. *Fat fucking chance*, I thought.

"Carla," Hector said, air-kissing one cheek, then the other. "It's so good to see you again." He pressed our tickets into her slender fingers.

"How many?"

He motioned over his shoulder. "Five."

"Five coming in," Carla said to the bouncer. She welcomed us with a wave of her arm.

Rachael, Jason, Mandy, and I slipped behind Hector, through the gate, and into the compound.

"Rock stars," Mandy said.

"Rock stars with Hector," I added. "Hey, Hector," I said, "is there a door person anywhere in the world you don't know?"

"Her brother is one of my patients," he said.

"If I had to grow up with her, I'd be one of your patients, too," Rachael said. She adjusted one of the plastic leis she has strung around her neck.

"Could I have another sip?" Mandy whispered, referring to the half-full bottle of G-spiked Gatorade the Porn Boys prepared for me before we left the house.

"Again?"   I   asked.

"That was hours ago."

"Remember what I told you about waiting." I pointed the neck of the bottle at her and impersonated the Ice Princess. "*I'm sorry, no.*" I patted her rear. Mandy and Jason's sexual antics had gotten to me, but I was getting over it. I had never been much at holding a grudge. Plus, it was difficult to stay angry with Mandy when she kept explaining to me what she was going to do to me later and augmenting that explanation with a brief demonstration. Besides, Rachael was more than making up for my thaw with arctic blasts emanating from her very cold shoulder.

The five of us started up the pathway leading to the pale-gray contemporary two-story house.

Hector leaned over to me and said, "Welcome to the home that crystal built."

"Now can I have that hit?" Mandy asked.

"Honestly, are you going to ask me every two minutes?"

"Honestly? Yes."

We stepped off the path and I handed her the bottle. "One sip. A *small* one."

She drank. "That's enough." I tugged at the bottom of the bottle.

Mandy stopped drinking but held on to the bottle. "Rachael's pissed at us, isn't she?"

"She's . . . we're, feeling kind of left out."

"I knew it. I told Jason. This isn't like me, really. This is a crazy place, such a crazy place. When we get back to Hector's I'm going to make it up to you. Her free hand slid down my stomach.

I didn't notice Rachael until she was right next to us. Her eyes shifted from Mandy's hand plunged down my jeans to the other one holding the bottle.

"I thought you were going to be more careful with that," she said, ostensibly referring to the G.

"I am." I turned to Mandy, who had the bottle up to her lips again.

"We should get to the party. *Now*," Rachael said.

"Okay," I said, snatching the bottle from Mandy.

I took a quick swig and poured the rest onto the ground.

We caught up with Hector and Jason just as they rounded the corner of the house. Every square inch of the broad deck surrounding the pool was jammed with people. Lights were mounted everywhere, spinning and playing across the crowd, the trees, the bay, and the pool, which had been put to good use by dozens of men and a few mostly naked women perched on their shoulders, arms over heads, swaying to Victor Calderone's steady, percussive grind.

"This is a house party?" Jason said. "Not where I come from."

Rachael gave me a satisfied look. Rachael put her hand on Jason's shoulder. His hand slid down her back and under the top of her shorts. *OK, fine.* I walked behind Mandy and wrapped my hands around her waist. She leaned back into me. A warm buzz like candle wax melted through me.

I was about to ask Hector exactly how much crystal one had to move in order pay for this kind of party, when a spotlight swung around and pointed up to the gently sloped roof of the house. There, arms outstretched, was perched a lithe, gold-lamé clad, drag queen in a Marilyn Monroe wig. The crowd hooted. She reached down and picked up a cardboard box overflowing with ghostly glowing bracelets, showering the crowd with them by the fistful. Jason caught a bunch and we put them on our heads like halos.

Across the bay, a bright-orange full moon broke the surface of the water. I tapped Mandy on the shoulder and pointed to it. She put her mouth to my ear and said, "Fantasy land."

"Got that right," I said. "How are you feeling?"

"Fantastic." She brought the palm of her hand to her forehead. "Kind of warm though. Might need a dip in the pool later."

Things were looking up. Victor Calderone dropped in a slamming remix of Toni Braxton's "Unbreak My Heart," jacking up the volume as he did. The preliminaries were over.

Mandy wiggled away from me, spinning circles, one hand waving over her head like a bull rider. "I love this song." She backed into Jason, who turned around and smiled at her. "Dance with me," she said, pulling him away from Rachael. "*Now.*"

Mandy pressed herself against Jason, ran her hands through his thick black hair and down his chest. Rachael backed away from them, throwing me a sarcastic smile. Her anger nailed me with the intensity of a shock wave. She stood there alone, her arms crossed, exuding displeasure.

"Come on, dance with me, baby," Mandy said to Jason. She tossed back her head and closed her eyes.

Jason brought his arms down to her waist and pulled her closer. "What do you call this?"

"Not dancing," she said, rubbing herself up and down Jason's chest and stomach. "This is." They drew the attention a small crowd, who formed a semi-circle around them, clapping time to the rhythm.

"Damn, girl," said Jason, laughing, "feeling pretty good, are we?"

Rachael looked around at the crowd and ground her jaw.

Mandy took Jason's hands and put them on her breasts.

Calderone looped the lead-in to the chorus, repeated it over and over, cranking the energy.

"You *go*, girl," said a bald-headed guy who bore a remarkable resemblance to Mr. Clean. Without looking back, Mandy pulled him to her, took his hands and placed them on Jason's shoulders, sandwiching herself in between. She yanked her shirt off and twirled it over her head. Mr. Clean worked his hands over her stomach and breasts. The three of them bent at the knees and ground down to the floor. To huge applause, Mandy pulled off Jason's shirt and began kissing his chest. More people noticed the threesome and drifted over. Two large men stepped in front of Rachael, jostling her out of the way.

She gave them a dirty look and walked over to me.

"Isn't this just lovely," she said.

I put my arm around her.

"Bad enough doing it in front of a few tweaked queens by the pool, but here? This is *not* okay," Rachael said in the same tone she used to reprimand the dogs at Big Bark.

I nodded in agreement. But the truth was, no one looked appalled. And I doubted Hector faced the slightest chance of humiliation. In fact, he would probably be immortalized as the guy who brought the fabulous hot straight couple to the party.

Mr. Clean put his hands under Mandy's arms and lifted her up off the ground. Jason wrapped Mandy's legs around his waist, thrusting against her. She undid the top button of her shorts, then reached forward and tried to unzip Jason's pants.

The song broke free to the chorus, the lights shifted from amber to harsh white. Mandy's legs dropped from Jason's hips, causing Mr. Clean to lose his balance and pitch backwards. He landed on the floor with Mandy on top of him, a tangle of arms and legs. He yelled something, drowned out by the music and the shouting. Jason knelt and tried to help them up, but Mandy was dead weight. Her head rested against her shoulder at an impossible angle.

Jason looked down at her. "Are you okay?"

Hector pushed through the crowd and dropped down to one knee, studying Mandy's face. Her eyes cleared for a moment, then rolled back in her head. "Help me," Hector said.

Jason and I each took an arm and we got Mandy up onto her feet. Her knees buckled and we just managed to catch her before she fell forward.

Mr. Clean yelled into my ear, "You better deal with that." We dragged her off the dance floor away from the lights and set her down against the trunk of a tree.

Jason squatted down next to her. "What's wrong with her?"

"It's G," I said.

"For fuck's sake, Nick," Rachael said.

Sweat dripped off my forehead. Dread jerked me sober.

"Mandy, you okay?" Jason said. She was drifting in and out, trying to speak.

Jason turned to Hector. "What do we do?"

Hector held Mandy's wrist, taking her pulse. "We need to get her to my place without attracting too much attention or we're all going to end up in jail. And if anyone asks, it's K, not G."

Mr. Clean came over and handed me her T-shirt. "She dropped this," he said. He bent over, resting both hands on his knees. "K-hole?" he asked.

I nodded.

"Here's something that'll help." He handed me a small plastic tube the size of a travel-sized container of toothpaste. "Cake frosting," he said. "The sugar will bring her out of it."

I couldn't help but wonder if the folks back at the Betty Crocker plant had heard that the fruit of their labor doubled as the antidote to a ketamine overdose. "Thanks," I said, and handed it to Hector.

"You should get her on her feet," he said. "I heard there're undercover cops."

"Thanks, we'll take it from here," Hector said.

Mr. Clean backed away. "The things we do for fun, huh?"

Hector waited until Mr. Clean was out of earshot, then threw the tube of frosting into bush.

"Give me a few seconds to talk to Carla. Put her shirt on. Do not let her fall asleep. Got it?"

I bent down next to Mandy and took her chin in my hand. Her head trembled, and, for a moment, I thought she was starting a seizure, until I realized it was my hand that was shaking uncontrollably. Jason and Rachael slipped Mandy's shirt over her head and passed her limp arms through each side.

Hector rushed back. "Let's go."

"Come on, Mandy, we're going to go now," Jason said.

Jason and I got her on her feet and draped her arms around our shoulders.

Out we went, taking small, shuffling steps past dozens of people still arriving. "Party of one," someone said, "coming through."

At the entrance to the property, we passed Carla, who shot a worried glance at Mandy. "Everything okay here?" she asked.

"She'll be fine," Hector said. "Just needs a little time to herself." Carla wished us luck, but also seemed very relieved to see us go.

The boardwalk appeared especially narrow and dark. The moon helped a bit, casting a soft glow along the path, but it was slow going, especially with Mandy stopping dead in her tracks every few steps. It was only a couple of hundred yards to Hector's house, but at this rate it would take forever.

Jason said to me, "Let's carry her." Jason and I locked arms to form a modified fireman's carry, slid them under Mandy and hoisted her up.

"Put your hands on our shoulders," Jason said.

Mandy sat motionless between us.

We were halfway to Hector's when Mandy let out a howling moan. Her body began to tremble.

"She's seizing," Hector said. "Hurry."

Jason and I broke into a trot. With Mandy's head bouncing against Jason's chest, we made the sharp right to the entrance to the house, squeezed through the front door, and deposited her on the living room sofa.

Tweaked and Chipper, wearing matching orange Speedos, stood in the kitchen. "Jesus," one of them said, "what happened?"

"G," Hector said.

"I warned her," the other said. "More than once."

Mandy was out cold. Hector tapped her on both cheeks and yelled, "Mandy. Mandy, *wake up.*"

She didn't respond.

"How about crystal?" Jason asked. He leaned over the arm of the sofa, breathing hard, staring down at her. "Won't that bring her out of it?"

Hector waved Jason off as he calculated Mandy's pulse rate. "Get me some ice in a towel." I ran to the fridge and emptied two ice trays into a beach towel, ran back, and handed it to Hector. "I need to get this under her head." Jason and I lifted Mandy up and Hector placed the towel-wrapped ice at the base of her neck.

Mandy's eyes opened again and then slammed shut.

"Now what?" Jason asked.

Hector puffed up his cheeks and exhaled. "We watch and we wait."

"Wait?" I said. "She needs to go to a hospital."

Hector shook his head. "St. Barts gets a ton of G overdoses. They won't do anything in a hospital we can't do here. The G suppresses your respiratory system. Stimulants make it worse, not better. She's fading in and out, which is a good sign. It will probably pass on its own."

"Probably?" Jason said.

I slumped down on the floor next to the sofa and dropped my head in my hands, rocking back and forth, the shame burning through me.

For the next hour, we watched and waited. Jason sat across the living room on an armchair, occasionally walking over to touch Mandy's hair. Every few minutes, Hector took Mandy's pulse. I watched the rise and fall of Mandy's stomach, willing her to keep breathing. The Porn Boys wandered back and forth from their room. For a while, Rachael sat at the end of the sofa, rubbing Mandy's feet, but on the Porn Boys' second or third trip, Rachael followed them. When she returned, she was wide-eyed and jumpy, pacing around the sofa and sighing a lot.

I was tempted to join them, but I couldn't shake a horrifying image of Mandy taking her last breath at the precise moment I touched my lips to a crack pipe. I sat on the floor staring at her calm face. Two or three times, it seemed Mandy might revive. She groaned and mumbled and shifted around, but then faded away. I watched her, my heart a pile driver, then checked Hector's expression, in vain, for some clue to her condition. The air in the room, the room itself, felt compressed.

"How long can this go on?" Jason asked.

"A few hours," Hector said.

"A few *hours*?" Jason said. "And you're sure we shouldn't get her to a hospital? I know you're concerned about your license and rep and all, but—"

"Hi," Mandy said. I pushed away from the sofa and nearly fell over.

"*Hi,*" she said again.

No one said anything.

"What's going on?"

I smiled, relief rushing through me like white-water rapids.

"How do you feel?" Hector asked.

"Can you help me sit?"

Hector and I slid her up onto one of the cushions of the sofa. Jason crossed the room in two long strides and hugged her. "You scared us to death, girl."

"What happened?" she said. She cradled Jason's head in her hands. "Last thing I remember we were at the party, dancing. A lot."

"It was the G," I said.

"Love that stuff." Mandy said. She looked around the room. "*What?*"

"You were out," Hector said.

"I was? I thought I was dreaming. Couple of times I could see you all, but it was like I was under water. Then the water got freezing cold." She reached behind her, removed the icy, wet towel, and dropped it on the floor. "No wonder." Mandy looked down at her chest. "Hey, my shirt's on inside out."

"Yeah, so is my stomach," I said.

"You were worried?"

"Just a little," Rachael said.

Mandy rubbed her eyes. "I feel like I took a long nap."

"Your nap started on the middle of the dance floor," Jason said.

"I'm so sorry," she said. "I'm fine now."

"We're going to the party, if you want to come back with us," Chipper said.

"You're kidding, right?" I said.

"Nah," Mandy said. "I'm up for it."

"I'm game if she is," Jason said.

"Seems a waste not to," Rachael said, shifting her weight from one foot to the other.

Everyone was gathered by the front door now, chuckling and jovial, as if nothing had happened.

I got up slowly. That thing Mr. Clean said came back to me.

"The things we do for fun," I said.

25

Bad Santa

We returned home from Fire Island and tumbled into a spectacular crash. An immense black shroud descended over me and Rachael, a grinding, relentless hopelessness. Our sleep-and-food-deprived bodies finally teamed up with our ravaged nervous systems and our bruised egos to let us have it, right in the old cerebellum. We slept constantly and never felt rested. The smallest task seemed insurmountable. Unread newspapers, still in their plastic sleeves, gathered on the table in the kitchen. Plants went un-watered. There was no food in the house. It was all I could do to drag myself to the phone and call in an order of Chinese food for delivery.

A couple of days after our return, Rachael, who'd been gnawing on Jason and Mandy's behavior on Fire Island like a junkyard dog, called Jason to tell him she thought he owed Hector an apology. Before he hung up on her, Jason managed to work into the conversation that he thought Rachael was a self-centered, pathetic cunt who couldn't even satisfy her own husband.

She didn't take it well.

I heard the sound of shattering glass and hurried down to the kitchen to find Rachael in a fetal position on the floor, uninjured, but crying as though she'd just severed an arm. A porcelain vase, a wedding present from my mother, was smashed on the tile floor. I managed to get her up and into bed but not until she told me, quite convincingly, that if I didn't find her some crystal, she was going to kill herself.

Wes, who'd started a home delivery service, sent someone over. The deliveries became frequent.

Big Bark's surge slowed to a trickle, probably a natural flattening of the growth curve encountered by every business. Rachael panicked, blamed everything on Anna's lack of management skill and became convinced that without her immediate intervention the business would fail, that we'd spend our golden years "eating cat food." About the same time, we had to come to terms with another inevitability, a competitor. Someone had opened a small facility across town. The business was no threat to Big Bark, which by now had developed a loyal customer base. Rachael, saw the development as both a threat and a personal insult. "I'm going to bury them," she said.

She began to spend a lot of time at Big Bark, including evenings and weekends, the crystal her constant companion. Rachael, once the ultimate pack leader, now sent the dogs into paroxysms of frantic, chaotic barking every time she set foot on the property.

At Rachael's insistence, I started covering more shifts. I lost all interest in participating in the management of the business or interacting with the customers, choosing instead to occupy myself with cleaning out the cages and scooping shit from the play yard, tasks which allowed me to remain sullen and uncommunicative.

Rachael and Anna had their first serious argument over whether to offer grooming services. Privately, Anna admitted to me the real problem was that she felt micro-managed and unappreciated, her authority undermined. She was finding it increasingly difficult to work with Rachael, who was more demanding and irrational. I kept it all from Rachael, terrified that she might overreact and fire Anna.

Rachael's ambitious plan to expand Big Bark and become the doyenne of doggy-dom now seemed as outlandish as it did grandiose. She seemed unable to relax, often leaping out of bed in an explosion of agitation. "I'm antsy," she'd say, a proclamation which was inevitably followed by a call to Wes.

Concerned about Rachael's state, I suggested she try yoga. One day, a substitute instructor named Hans, who looked and acted like a direct descendant of a Nazi Brown Shirt, forced Rachael into a challenging pose and something in her neck gave way. She couldn't get out of bed for days.

An MRI turned up a degenerated disc. Surgery was an option, though not one recommended by the doctors, at least not yet. For her pain, she was prescribed Percocet, and, for acute flare-ups, Oxycontin.

One day, we heard a news report about Oxycontin abuse, how kids and housewives in the Midwest were smashing the pills into powder and snorting them. Sounded good to us. It worked, temporarily taking the edge off Rachael's anxiety and my despondency. Between Rachael's increasing appetite and my dipping into her stock, she quickly ran through her prescriptions and took to pressuring me to press our friends for pills. "Did you ask him?" became her mantra. Hector began to fill in the gaps with scripts he mailed to us from New York.

Our change in fortune turned nearly biblical. We weren't beset by locusts, but our house suffered a termite infestation that, literally, ate the foundation away from under us. In the kitchen, all the supporting joists and the subfloor had to be replaced. It was a miracle, the contractors said, that the entire room hadn't collapsed. For the next several weeks, our kitchen looked like the entrance to a mineshaft.

Early one morning, we received a phone call from Wes informing us that Trevor had had been taken to George Washington Hospital Center. We rushed over and were shocked to find him in intensive care, breathing with the aid of a ventilator. Wes and Trevor had just returned from a week in Provincetown. They'd been, as Wes put it, out and about, nothing out of the ordinary, a euphemism for not much sleep and plenty of crystal. Ever since they returned, Trevor had been feeling a little run down. That morning, he'd awoken to a raging fever, unable to lift his head. The doctors had diagnosed a serious systemic infection which had attacked his body and, in particular, the lining of his heart. Trevor had been HIV positive for years, but this was the first time he'd been ill. Now, with his immune system seriously compromised, things were touch and go.

"Touch and go? What does that mean?" Rachael asked. Wes broke down crying. A friend of ours, an anesthesiologist at the hospital, swung by and looked in on Trevor. He took us to the side. He hadn't wanted to say it in front of Wes, but he'd seen similar cases over the years. It didn't look good. The risk of further infection to him was so great that they wouldn't even allow any visitors. Best we could do is steal a couple of quick glances though the door at Trevor, lying there, the bellows-like ventilator his only companion.

On the way back home, Rachael stared out of the car window. "I've known him since I was fifteen years old. If he dies, I don't know what I'm going to do."

My former swagger had turned into a sulking shuffle. Lying in bed with all the shutters closed, I would fantasize about running away, then punish myself for allowing myself such thoughts, for being irresponsible, ungrateful, and a coward.

On the Saturday before Christmas, we swung open the gates of Big Bark to reveal our fourth annual canine Christmas. The compound was festooned in red ribbon and glittery stars that dangled from the ceiling. There were stuffed reindeer and elves. There was a three-foot high candy-cane shaped canister crammed full of homemade dog treats. There were cinnamon-scented tea lights. There was our backdrop, a six-foot artificial Christmas tree, adorned with tinsel and blinking lights and chew-toy ornaments. There was our friend, a former White House photographer, with her six-thousand dollar-state-of-the art digital camera. There was Frank Sinatra's voice wafting Christmas carols from the stereo we had lugged from home.

And there was Santa.

I sat surrounded by dog crates on a folding chair in the center of the main playroom. My rented Santa outfit was too big around the waist and too tight in the shoulders. The tassel, which dangled down from the cap, kept tickling my ear. The beard itched. The boots were hot.

At noon, Rachael ducked her head into the room. She said, "You look adorable."

I didn't feel adorable. But we had it all worked out. Ten-to-fifteen dogs. It would be over in an hour—hour and a half, tops.

We had miscalculated. By twelve-thirty, there were twenty-five dogs. By one o'clock, there were more than thirty. And they just kept coming: dachshunds and beagles and wolfhounds and corgis, collies and bloodhounds and boxers and Yorkies. Some had come from as far as Atlanta, dressed as elves and reindeer and yes, even Santa.

Rachael directed the owners to the punch bowl and started a sign-up sheet for dogs to get their picture taken with Santa. First up was Calvin, one of our regulars. Calvin was a sweet and mellow basset hound, owned by a high-strung attorney. So many of our customers were high-strung attorneys. I rose from my chair to greet them.

In my most avuncular Santa voice I said, "Merry Christmas, Calvin."

Calvin backed away. Then he growled. Calvin never growled.

I dropped to one knee so he could get a better look at me. In my own voice, I said, "Hey, it's me, buddy."

Calvin responded with an impressive stream of projectile diarrhea.

Calvin's reaction to me in my Santa outfit may have been the most pungent of the day, but not the most extreme. Little lap dogs snarled at me. Others paralyzed by fear and had to be dragged over, their paws splayed out and gripping the floor in panic. Some broke into a jittery canter around the perimeter of the room, drooling and not making eye contact. There was lots of vomit. The dogs we managed to cajole into my lap either sat there squirming like they were getting shock therapy or ducked their trembling heads into my armpits.

We had figured on five minutes per portrait. It was taking twenty. The dogs and their owners were stacking up like jets on a busy runway. A cranky energy crept through the place. And I don't just mean the dogs. Our customers were accustomed to getting their way. They began to ask, "How much longer do you think it might *be.*"

At first, I laughed it all off. Sometime around two o'clock, I began to take things personally. Sometime around three o'clock, I began to hate. I hated our customers, for their whining and sense of entitlement. I hated Rachael for her manipulative selfishness. I even hated the dogs for turning on me. Most of all, I hated myself for being the kind of guy who always went along, always the nice guy, like a clown. Like Santa.

By three-thirty, we still had a dozen more dogs to shoot. By four, I wanted to shoot the dogs. By five, Rachael had placed phone calls to arrange two critical deliveries. First to the liquor store for more rum for the punch; second, to Wes. They arrived at about the same time.

I shuffled over to Rachael in my hot Santa boots and poked her in the shoulder.

She said, "Now?"

I said, "*Hell yes.*"

She took one look at me and decided not to argue. I slipped the baggie into my giant Santa pocket, grabbed a half-full bottle of rum and headed to the bathroom.

I had begun the day as Saint Nick. I emerged from the bathroom as the nightmare before Christmas.

I plunked back down in the chair and surveyed the remaining dogs. My eyes landed on Oscar, a fat dachshund whose belly dragged the ground when he walked. Oscar's perpetually depressed owner kept him on a balanced diet of M&Ms and Skittles. She held him up like an offering. She said, "He's been waiting *so* long."

For the first time in hours I smiled. I said, "Of course."

Oscar's owner deposited him in my lap where Oscar settled in, resigned, like an old man in a Barcalounger.

The photographer said, "Finally, an easy one."

I could blame what I did next on lots of things: the meth, the rum, frustration, fatigue. The truth is as simple as it is inexcusable. I wanted to inflict my pain on something, on anything. With one hand I stroked Oscar's head. With the other I searched underneath Oscar's ample belly until I found what I was looking for, a raw spot where it made contact with the ground. Just as the photographer was about to take the picture, I squeezed.

Oscar yelped, leapt off my lap, and landed with a sound like a plucked, wet chicken dropped onto a concrete floor.

My memories of what happened next are disjointed, but distinct: the boxer and the Weimaraner that latched on to either end of a stuffed reindeer until they had dismembered it before turning on each other; the Labrador that brought down the Christmas tree, then careened around the facility with frenzied eyes and a chew-toy ornament lodged in his jaws; the candy-cane canister that smashed to the ground, scattering a slick of dog treats across the linoleum; the primeval snarls as dogs leapt into the fray; and the shrieks of owners, scampering around after their pets in futile little circles.

I stood by the door to the bathroom, taking it all in. Just a guy wearing an ill-fitting Santa outfit, holding a mostly empty bottle of rum. I was bad Santa, all right. The dogs knew it and so did I. What I didn't know was that I was on my way to being a lot of other bad things.

26

The Road to Nowhere

Trevor didn't die. Somehow, he fought off his infection and began to recover. About a week after he was admitted to the hospital, they took him off the ventilator. On the first day he was allowed visitors, Rachael and I spent several hours at his bedside. Trevor was pale and thin, but in good spirits. Rachael sat next to him, holding his hand, smiling, visibly relieved. Though the ventilator tube was out of his throat, it would be several days before Trevor could speak. In the meantime, he communicated by means of a Ouija board, which Wes had dug up somewhere.

"How appropriate," Rachael said.

Trevor moved the heart-shaped planchette around the alphabet printed on the board, slowly piecing together a request: "Dish the dirt."

Rachael laughed. "You almost go and die on me and the first thing you want to do is catch up on gossip?"

Trevor nodded.

"Well, okay then." Rachael launched in on a far-ranging debriefing, including the latest news regarding Big Bark, the precipitous decline of the NASDAQ, the latest regarding Monica Lewinsky and Bill Clinton, and who had broken up with whom.

Trevor pointed to Rachael, then to me. He shrugged.

"Us?" Rachael said, not looking at me. "We're fine."

Trevor guided the planchette quickly. B-U-L-L

"You just worry about yourself right now," I said, anxious to change the subject.

A few weeks later, while Rachael was at Big Bark with Anna installing a new point-of-sale software system, Trevor and Wes paid me an unexpected visit. Trevor had been out of the hospital about a week. He had put on weight and was back doing short shifts at Beck and Call. I invited them into the parlor where they took seats on the sofa. I sat across from them in an armchair. Wes and Trevor scooted so close to each other they seemed joined at the hip.

"We're worried about you and Rachael," Wes said.

"And we're not alone," Trevor said.

"I know you guys are having a tough time," Wes said.

"It's more than that," Trevor said. "She's headed to a very bad place."

"She's so volatile and distant, there's just no warmth there, no humor. She's not the Rachael we knew," Wes said.

Trevor leaned forward, "And this bit about Mandy and the G. If I hear that story one more time, I'm going to lose it. She beats you with it like a drum. And you never say anything."

I stared at the coffee table. "I've noticed."

"You need to do more than notice," Trevor said. "You need to consider your responsibility in all this."

This I didn't expect. "Me?"

"You seem miserable. Lost."

"It's hard to watch," Wes said.

"Let's get down to it," Trevor said. "It's the crystal, and now the pain killers. I'm not sure about you, but she's addicted, for sure. And it's affecting your lives."

"And your friendships," Wes said.

Trevor nodded. "Have you noticed we don't get together as much as we used to? There was a reason we didn't go with you to Fire Island. We knew how it would be. We're headed in different directions. This thing that happened to me was a wakeup call. It should be to you, too. Most of your friends are scaling back from that life. Moving on. But you guys, you just keep going deeper." Secretly, I hoped someone might intervene regarding Rachael, but I didn't expect to be considered part of the problem. After all, I spent most of my time taking care of her, didn't I? "I admit, we've had a bad run. But I seem to recall a certain party at your house, the night we met, you serving up bumps like bon-bons. Out of our minds in Montreal and Mykonos. That time at Hombre. Provincetown. Not to mention your business, Wes. Seems a bit hypocritical, doesn't it?"

"I'm getting out," Wes said. "While I still can."

"Hate to say it," Trevor said, "but most of your wounds are self-inflicted. When we're toothless oldtrolls, we'll sit around, dig out our old club wear that doesn't fit anymore and talk about the good old days. But let's face it, that life is a calculated risk." He tapped the coffee table with his index finger. "We all danced right up to the edge. Rachael has gone over. You're right behind her. I warned you guys about doing crystal at work, about smoking it, and you did it. Then I warned you about bringing that couple to Morning Party and theG and Hector, too."

I said, "Hector is pretty, well—"

Trevor punched his knee with his balled-up fist. "Hector is next. I was in New York last month, and I saw him out at Body and Soul, a Sunday evening, dancing like a freak. I'd hate to be one of his Monday morning patients."

"We don't want to see that happen to Rachael," Wes said. "Or to you. I don't know you as well as Rachael. I don't think anyone really knows you, especially not lately. Ever since Fire Island, it feels like you checked-out."

"If you keep on living your life like this," Trevor said, "sooner or later, you're going to be the big Greek tragedy."

Wes glanced at Trevor, looking pained. "Besides, we don't want to be fifty and still hanging on to that kind of life."

"Unless she does something about it, Rachael isn't going to see fifty," Trevor said.

"That's a little dramatic, Trevor," Wes said.

"Don't get soft on me now; we've talked about this a million times. Maybe it's dramatic. But it's also true. Rachael is on the road to nowhere."

Wes looked me right in the eyes. "We're here to tell you that we'll support you in any way we can, but we think Rachael needs to consider some drastic changes in her life."

"Drastic?"

"Say what you mean, Wes," Trevor said. "She needs professional help. And yes, Wes is right, you'll get all the support in the world from us and your other friends if you two decide to tackle this thing."

"And if we don't?"

Trevor looked down at his feet. "Well then, it's safe to say you won't have many real friends left."

I dug my elbows into my thighs. "What if I can't get her to do it?"

There was silence.

"If she won't change, you save yourself," said Wes, gentle Wes, emphatic and with an edge to his voice. "You try your best, but the day you know it won't work, you disappear."

Trevor put his hand on Wes's knee and nodded.

Wes continued, "By disappear, I don't mean—"

"Got it, Wes," I said, my head cradled in my arms.

No one needed to explain the meaning of disappearing, not to me. I'd read the book and seen the movie. Now, I had to write the sequel.

That night, I called Rachael and told her that she should consider rehab. I had expected the line to go dead. Instead, she agreed. She felt out of control, like our lives were spiraling down. Rachael's only conditions: that she could choose the facility, and that I would participate fully and support her in her recovery. Of course. Anything, I said.

After several days of research on the Internet, a search that ruled out several prominent facilities, including Hazelden ("Minnesota in January? You *must* be kidding.") and the Betty Ford Clinic ("I am *not* spending a month in The Valley of the Dolls"), Rachael found the perfect place. She would kick her habit at a facility named Tradewinds, frequented by celebrities, caressed by the steady breezes and glorious beaches of Antigua.

She was aware of the unpleasant aspects of rehab, but the setting allowed Rachael a more palatable vision of what might await, one in which she sat on a sun-dappled veranda sporting Jackie-O sunglasses and a scarf, her fingers soaking in a solution of hibiscus water and honeybee emollients as she awaited her manicure.

A few phone calls and a ten-thousand-dollar wire transfer later, things were all set.

Now, all I had to do was get her there.

The Nudge

I came down from our bedroom to the office rubbing the sleep from my eyes. Rachael was where I left her hours ago, in front of the computer, wearing a white waffle-weave bathrobe and fuzzy slippers, making minute and undetectable changes to an ad she was designing for Big Bark.

"You *cannot* still be tinkering with that," I said.

Her eyes stayed fixed on the screen. A small bag of crystal with a blue plastic pen cap shoved in it lay next to the keyboard.

"This is not tinkering. See how unbalanced it looks? The design is totally fucked. And the copy is a disaster."

She was hoarse. I swung around to get a look at her. I had never seen her this haggard. Well, maybe once at the Black Party, but the lighting at Roseland had been more flattering than the lifeless early-December rays angling through our office window. I looked at the time displayed at the bottom right-hand corner of the computer screen—8:12 a.m.

"Why don't you let me take a shot at it later?" I suggested. "We have to leave by eleven for the airport and —"

She slammed the top of the desk with the mouse. "I know what time it is. I have to get this done. I have to get everything done." She swiveled around in her chair. The circles under her eyes were black gashes. "Just leave me alone and let me get this finished so I can do the other five hundred things I have to do."

"*Fine*," I said. I dug the pen cap deep into the crystal and did a bump. A big one.

Before we left for the airport, we followed through on our commitment to perform a house-wide narcotic exorcism. In room after room, we opened cabinets and drawers and were shocked at the volume and variety of what we found: bumpers in the bedside tables, residue-encrusted baggies on and under the desk, rusty single-edged razor blades in the silverware drawer (left over from those comparatively innocent days of snorting cocaine), and the mother lode, the junk drawer next to the kitchen sink, the holding and re-supply area.

As I watched the last baggie of crystal swirl down the toilet, I felt relieved. For now. The truth was, I was still high and not sure how I was going to feel about it later, after she was gone, when the inevitable crash came, when it would be just me and this big, empty, old house.

I loaded her luggage, all carefully packed days ago, in the car. It was eleven thirty. We were cutting it close. The late departure didn't help settle my nerves.

Finally, halfway to the airport I began to relax.

"You *are* coming to get me, right?" she asked.

"I'll be there."

"It's really important to be there."

"I've already made my reservations. Already paid. We've gone over all this, remember?"

"Right. Oh fuck."

"What is it?"

"My passport. I think I left it in the office."

She rummaged through her purse. "I think I left it," she said with more certainty.

"Are you sure? I thought you put it in your purse." I glanced at the digital clock on the dash. If we turned back, we'd never make the flight.

"It's not here," she said, her voice full of anguish and edge. She took her purse and dumped everything onto the floor.

"What the hell are you doing?" I was on the verge of panic, too. My mind was already running through scenarios. Missing this flight meant missing her connection in San Juan, the last one of the day. The thought of trying to repeat this process the next day was too much to bear, especially since we'd flushed all the crystal. Once Rachael crashed, I wouldn't be able to get her out of the house much less onto a plane bound for rehab. Any delay would give her an excuse to call off the whole damn thing.

Rachael was bent over, rifling through the contents of her purse. I heard the rustling and snap of keys, makeup cases, and paper.

"Any luck?" I said, trying to sound calm.

"I can't believe this." She took her wallet and turned it upside down. Hundreds of dollars dumped onto her lap and spilled onto the floor. "It was on the desk. I saw it yesterday."

"Me too. Maybe Trevor or Wes can go by the house and meet us at the airport."

She shrieked and stomped both her feet to the floor. "*Forget it.* This is obviously not meant to be."

My stomach drew up into a tight, dark knot. "Just calm down."

Rachael straightened up and turned to me, crying. "I can't do this. Who was I kidding? I need a vacation, not rehab. For ten thousand dollars, we could have a hell of a vacation, right? I hear the beaches in Antigua are beautiful."

I was about to lose all the initiative. Honestly, a vacation on a tropical island sounded pretty good to me, too. Where *was* that passport? I'd seen it yesterday, made a mental note to make sure she took it with her. In fact, I'd picked it up, held it in my hands.

"Oh hell," I said.

"What?"

"Look in the glove compartment."

Rachael opened the hinged door and removed her passport. "For Christ's sake. Like we don't have enough stress?"

"I put it there yesterday," I said. "So we wouldn't forget."

She tossed the passport in her purse and leaned back in her seat. "The thing is, I'm scared shitless."

"I don't blame you. But do you want to keep living like this? I mean, look at yourself." This, I knew, was my last line of defense.

Rachael flipped down the sun visor and angled the mirror mounted on the back of it. She turned her head from side to side. The sky had turned overcast, the light as thin and gray as she.

She flipped the visor away. "All right." She began, one by one, putting things back into her purse. "Let's do this thing."

28

Love Letters in the Sand

Dateline: December, 2000, Tradewinds

<u>Day five</u>

Nick:

So sorry about the rather desperate-sounding phone call when I arrived, but I have to say—this was such a mistake. First thing they did was ransack my suitcase. My suitcase! As if I hadn't done up every drug I could get my hands on before I arrived. Then, they put me in some sort of holding pen. That's when I bolted and called you.

Anyway, after they managed to wrench the phone out of my hand, they stuck me in a medically supervised isolation for three nights to wean me off the Percocet so I wouldn't go into seizures. Three sleepless nights. Then, I crashed so hard they had to wake me and force me to eat. By the way, I weighed in at ninety-four pounds. I must have looked like a lemur hanging from a tree in Madagascar. They take a picture of you when you arrive. That's one photo I NEVER want to see.

It's pretty here, but rehab is rehab. No leaving the grounds (not that there's anywhere to go), breakfast at 7 a.m. sharp, morning group, lunch at noon, afternoon group, dinner at 5:30, evening meeting, lights out at 10 p.m. Rules and meetings—meetings and rules. I can already recite the fucking twelve steps backwards and forwards. They don't trust you for shit. Wes sent me a lovely care package and they went through it and confiscated the goddamn cologne because of the alcohol content. Figures they'd worry about me abusing the only drug I've never been interested in.

The other inmates are a trip. So successful and so fucked up. Heirs to fortunes, investment bankers, high-end hookers, you name it. Guess what? Compared to these people, I'm an addict lightweight! This tiny little girl from Texas, I swear she can't weigh but eighty pounds, has been shooting crystal and slugging down 50 Percocets a day. 50! You know how competitive I am. Had I known that was humanly possible, I would have gone for the record.

Yesterday, this high-powered corporate attorney/alcoholic checked herself out after only eighteen days. Said she was sick of all the rules and restrictions. The counselors predicted she'd relapse before she hit the airport.

I don't know if I can do this for a whole month. I haven't been able to call myself an addict yet,

*but there's no doubt I'm a big old mess. I'm
trying not to worry about things back home,
how you're doing—the business. Trying my
best to 'Let go and let God.' I miss you so
much it hurts. I've already started counting the
days.*

*Now that they've entrusted me with a pen, on
the condition that I won't jam it into myself or
anyone else, I promise to write.*

Love,

Shaky Spice

P.S. How are you doing?

How was I doing? Pretty damn well.

Things at Big Bark were good again. Anna, freed
from Rachael's oversight, enjoyed having things back in
her control. Sales were up, customers were happy and so
was Anna. Without the pressure and drama, I actually
liked spending time there. The official word was that
Rachael was undergoing treatment for her back injury.
But I'm sure Anna knew better.

I was feeling better physically, too. After Rachael
left, I crashed for three days, hardly getting out of bed
except to eat. Gradually, my nerves and my body began
to mend. I was relieved to find that, with the junk drawer
now full of nothing more tempting than Chinese takeout
menus, I wasn't craving anything. I fell into my
own routine: the gym, long walks, cooking big meals
for myself, movies with friends. I dusted off my drums
and began to play again. It was a new kind of normal.

I made an effort to reconnect with some of the people who had drifted away. My childhood friend, Gary, came to town to visit his mother for the holidays and brought along his toddler twins and a four-year-old. We spent the afternoon watching them create inventive ways to endanger themselves.

"Don't know how you do it, Gary," I said. I pulled a lamp cord out of the little girl's mouth.

"Not much choice in the matter. You just do it. Allan! *Allan.* Don't throw the chess pieces." He sighed. "Christie and I spend most of our time reacting. Raising kids doesn't give you much time to reflect. Sometimes, that's a good thing."

"Are things good with Christie? You happy?"

"She's a great mom. I love my kids." He shrugged. "The rest just happens."

Day eleven

Nick:

Don't get me wrong, this is the hardest thing I've ever done, but the sight of the sun setting behind the cliff over the cove is transcendent. There's no way you can witness it and feel that there isn't something out there bigger than yourself and whatever that thing is must have had a hand in creating it. Isn't that a trip, coming from the daughter of a dyed-in-the-wool-atheist-intellectual Jew? Every evening after our last group session, Arnold (the cocaine addicted chemist), and I sit under the gazebo overlooking the cliff and meditate. Arnold claims that the light of the

*setting sun stimulates the pituitary glands. I'm
not sure why you'd want to have your pituitary
glands stimulated, but Arnold's worth about fifty
million dollars and claims to have produced a
new, more potent version of crack, so I'm willing
to go along.*

*That's my life these days. The rest of the world is
a distant echo. I have no idea what's going on out
there and, frankly, I don't have time to care.*

Love

Miss Mess

I spent a quiet Christmas with my mother at our
house. It was pleasant, free from the subtle but ever-
present tension when she and Rachael were around each
other. After dinner she helped me with the dishes.

"I never wanted to say it," she said, "but I could
see this coming. I've been around alcoholics enough to see
the signs. They can be so charming and exciting. And if
you've got a nurturing streak, you just want to take care
of them. I hope what they teach her sticks. It did for your
father. He's a different person." She sighed. "Lot of good
it did me, though. You'd think I'd have learned my lesson
by now," she said, referring to her current husband, with
whom she had recently separated after he'd fallen off the
wagon following eight years of sobriety.

"We sure know how to pick them," I said.

She handed me the large, oval platter. "Anyway, if
you're lucky, maybe Rachael will be a different person,
too." She caught herself. "I didn't mean it to come out like

that. It's just that I've always made an effort with her, and she's kept me at a distance."

"She's got a thing about family. Hers, mine, and everyone else's."

"Sometimes family is everything."

Well, almost everything. About a week after Rachael left for Antigua, Trudie called. She'd heard about Rachael through the grapevine and was checking in to see how things were going and to get her address so she could write. We began to speak on the phone frequently. She was a good listener, and I found myself opening up to her.

"Too bad you don't live closer," I said one evening after we'd talked for more than an hour. "I'd buy you lunch."

"Baltimore's not that far. But maybe that wouldn't be such a good idea."

"Why not? I thought you've sworn off men."

"I have. Many times."

"It's just lunch."

"I don't think we should be having just anything. Not even lunch. *Boys.*"

Turns out the last man Trudie had a serious relationship with had been to rehab for cocaine and alcohol.

"I know the drill," she said. "Rest up and get yourself ready because when she gets home is when it starts getting tough. Don't try to wing it. You'll need a plan. Do you have a plan?"

I didn't have a clue, much less a plan. In search of one, I turned to my father. He and I hadn't had much contact for years. His sober lifestyle hadn't seemed like a good fit with mine. But now, who better to impart some wisdom regarding abstinence than someone with almost twenty years of it under his belt?

He was compassionate, but direct.

"The hell with a plan. There's a good reason they say to take it one day at a time. At first, that's about as far out as you can see. A lot less, especially early on. Don't get all grandiose with timelines; you're just setting yourself up to fail. Remember, when it comes to not getting high, failure is *always* an option."

Fair enough, but I wanted something that felt a little more tangible than simply clinging on, day to day. I found that something, courtesy of Trevor. Just a few days before leaving for Antigua, I went to dinner at Beck and Call. Afterwards, sitting at the bar, over several glasses of red wine, we formulated a strategy.

"One year. Anything less than a year of sobriety is trivial," he said. "Anything more than a year will seem overwhelming. A year. That's long enough to break the patterns and really change her behavior. It'll be over before you know it. Everyone will be so supportive, you'll see. Besides," he swirled the wine around in his goblet, "we can all stand to back off some. Maybe it's time we all grew up a little."

Trevor's optimism was an effective pairing with his Cabernet. After all, a year would fly by, wouldn't it? Trevor was right, how much longer could we keep behaving like twenty-five-year-old circuit boys? I pictured our friends, gathered as a big family around a long, candlelit table. We exchange warm and witty banter. Rachael is radiant as she watches Trevor carve a giant roasted something-or-another on an ornate serving platter, the same one on which she used to serve cocaine. Next, I flash to us all sitting at the concert hall at the Kennedy Center, clutching our playbills, marveling at the brilliance of the evening's performance, rising to applaud as we cast knowing, satisfied glances to each other, feeling urbane and adult in our fine clothes and our new lifestyle.

Then, I glanced down at Trevor's wine glass. From what I understood of recovery doctrine, addicts, even ones with a disdain for alcohol, couldn't sit around and sip wine. A buzz was a buzz, and a buzz would lead to impaired judgment, relapse, and ruin. The consequences of a truly sober lifestyle, even a temporary one, constricted my stomach like a tourniquet.

Trevor must have seen the change in my expression.

"What is it?" he asked. "More wine?"

I held out my empty glass. "Yes. Please. Quite a bit more."

Day nineteen

Nick:

Get this: at yoga today (twice a week, poolside, taught by a real yogi, not Hans the storm trooper), something happened, like a switch flipped. For about fifteen minutes I was (ready for this?) at peace. I don't know how else to describe it. Minutes passed and I was without need, want, craving, worry, or anger. Susan, my roommate, saw it in my face and described my expression as blissful. Next thing I knew, I was actually looking forward to the next meeting. I *finally admitted to being an addict—in front of the whole damn group. Everyone applauded and I cried and cried.*

Something is happening to me here, something I didn't expect and can't explain. It appears that I am getting it as they say, coming to realize how out of control and selfish I've been.

Speaking of getting it—I'm so horny I could pop, and I'm not alone. There are unauthorized hook-ups going on all over the place. Susan (the very cute sailboat skipper) and I have come to rely on long make out sessions and furious groping to pass the time after lights out. Both of us are too reliant on the high hard one to get much relief from second base, but it's better than nothing. Under different circumstances, I'd recommend that you, she, and I check into a hotel with a few hits of X, but that's definitely not standard operating procedure for recovering addicts. Still, the idea is not entirely without merit.

I don't know where all this is leading. I'm beginning to see how fruitless my efforts to control everything and everyone in my life have been, how I've masked my pain and fear with drugs and possessions and other crap that I thought would make me happy. I'm seeing the same patterns in the other inmates, many of whom are incredible people—really special. I can't wait for you to meet some of them. Nicky, I hope it's not too late for me to turn my life around. I'm on to something here. I'm just not quite sure what it is yet.

You'll be here soon. Maybe we can figure it out together?

Love,

Randy Rachael

Outtakes

"Her outtake session will be over in a few minutes," said Ms. Wells, Tradewind's senior counselor. "She should be packed and ready to go, so I'll have her meet you right here. Why don't you just have a seat and relax." Her crisp, authoritative manner, lovely chocolate-hued skin, and brilliant smile got my attention. And commanded my obedience. I swallowed hard, found the nearest seat in the waiting area, a cream-colored folding chair, and sat.

Her smile was compassionate yet unsettling. She shook her head, almost imperceptibly. Had I done something wrong? She pointed to a large, overstuffed leather sofa a few feet away. "Wouldn't you be more comfortable over there?"

"Of course." I moved over to the sofa.

"There, that's better. In fact, it's the best seat in the entire facility. Fabulous view of the grounds."

I followed her gaze across the room to a long bank of French doors, framed by sun-dappled hibiscus and bougainvillea. Beyond them, across a short stretch of lush grass, lay a white wooden gazebo with several white chairs arranged in a semi-circle underneath. Past the gazebo, the ground dropped away, reappearing several hundred yards away as steep, rocky cliff.

"Beautiful setting." I said. "That must help."

Ms. Wells looked off into the distance. "We need all the help we can get." Her attention snapped back to me. "So, any questions? Things that weren't covered in the session?" she asked, referring to the debriefing I and five other family members of *guests*, as they were referred to by the staff, had received, designed to prepare us for what to expect from our sobered-up loved ones.

"I suppose the obvious one: How is she doing?"

Ms. Wells took a step closer. She put both hands on her hips. "I must say she was in pretty bad shape when she got here. Physically, she was frail and a bit anemic, too. We're used to that, especially with crystal meth abusers. Many of our guests squeeze in one more bender before they get here and show up a wreck. The withdrawal from the opiates is not pleasant, not as dangerous as alcohol, but very uncomfortable. And we had to sort out the pain associated with her back problems from the temporary symptoms of her withdrawal. Physically, she's come back rather quickly, as you'll see. She's able to manage the discomfort in her back using anti-inflammatories now."

"That great, right?"

"Yes. But I'm more concerned about Rachael's attitude."

I winced.

"Specifically, her issues with authority and control. Early on, we had some problems with her challenging the rules. I believe you received an unauthorized phone call the night she arrived?"

I nodded.

"Very insistent and demanding. Initially, there was quite a bit of that sort of resistance. She's come around. Rachael is fully engaged in her sobriety, very enthusiastic. We just need to be sure that she doesn't get overconfident. A little humility goes a long way in the recovery process."

A humble Rachael, willing to give up control to a higher power?

"There's another issue we should face," she said.

I wasn't sure what she was going to say, but I was certain I wasn't going to like it.

"There's a much higher instance of relapse in households in which the addict's partner abuses drugs or alcohol. I understand you used drugs together?" Which I interpreted as: "You spineless, drug-addled bastard."

"That's all over," I said, trying to sound assuring.

"Good, I'm glad to hear it, Nick. She's going to need all the support she can get, especially from you." Ms. Wells smiled. "We've seen more difficult cases than Rachael do very well. Just don't get snowed by her bravado. There's a fragile little girl under there."

"I know she's trying. And when Rachael tries, she usually gets what she wants."

"Controlling the outcome. It's a common trait among addicts." She sighed. "Anyway, just take it a day at a time. She's excited to see you. Been talking about nothing else for days. I'll say goodbye before you leave."

Outside, a hummingbird with iridescent-blue highlights flitted among the thick patch of flowers and shrubs surrounding the gazebo. I opened the door and walked out to join it. From there, I could see the base of the cliff, anchored by a desolate, white sand cove, the same one Rachael had written about.

I sensed her presence before I saw her. There she was, in silhouette, backlit by the sun. Her hair was longer, well past her shoulders, and the humid air had caused it to curl. The sun filtered through, creating red and sparkly highlights. Now, she was close enough for me to see her face, and I stopped mid-breath. She glowed with health. The extra weight had restored her features. She was smiling, her brilliant white teeth emphasized by her tan. Three more steps and she was on me, her head sliding under my chin, her arms circling my back. She squeezed me hard. I put one hand on the top of her head and the other on the small of her back and pressed her to me. She smelled of jasmine.

We stood there swaying, not saying anything. I was transported back to Miami Beach, that night on the dance floor of the Warsaw.

I broke the silence. "You look fantastic."

"Clean living."

"Everyone says hello, and how proud of you they are."

"I've got a lot to tell you. I don't really know where to start."

"Start."

"Not just yet." She took her hand, cupped it over my crotch and squeezed.

"Hold up," I said, looking around. "I doubt that's allowed."

Rachael tugged me towards the building. "I don't care. I've been following the goddamn rules for twenty-seven-and-a-half days. If I don't get laid I'm going to explode or get high."

"Where are we going?" I asked.

"My room."

We crossed the lawn to a door. I tried not to think about the fact that Rachael was not even out of rehab and already breaking the rules. The room was clean and institutional. There were a couple of single beds, each with a swiveling reading light mounted to the wall behind it, two bedside tables, and two small desks and chairs.

Rachael backed me toward the nearest bed, moaning all the way.

"Are you sure this is okay?" I asked.

She unzipped my jeans and slid her hand down on me. "Don't worry," she said, breathless. She dropped her shorts and got on the bed. "All the other inmates have left, and the counselors are at a staff meeting."

"Just give it to me, would you?"

"Sure know how to romance a guy."

"Plenty of time for that later. Believe me, it won't take long."

She was right. It was over in a minute. Rachael moaned once, then collapsed back on the bed, her face damp and flushed.

"Jesus," she said. "That was hot."

For her, maybe.

I pulled up my pants. "I guess I'll be able to deduct that one from my taxes."

"Very funny. Now, get me out of this wacky place," she said. "I need to be home."

A few minutes later, Rachael and I walked through the main lobby, wheeling her luggage. Parked in the circular driveway was a beat-up gray Mercedes cab, beside which stood Ms. Wells.

"She doesn't look happy," I said.

"What's she going to do?" Rachael said. "Sentence me to another twenty-eight days?"

Ms. Wells motioned to the car. "Your cab," she said. "He's been waiting a while." She cocked her head ever so slightly as her eyes played across Rachael's face, studying and probing. I saw how these two must have gone at each other over the last month, like chess champions packing AK47s.

"I needed some extra help," Rachael said. With one foot out the door, Rachael was poking Ms. Wells with a stick.

Ms. Wells paused a beat. "I thought we'd gone over the outtake procedure. I would have had one of our staff move your bags to the waiting area."

"I didn't see anyone. Besides, it only took a minute. Right, Nick?"

It was one thing for Rachael to get her digs in, but I didn't like being used as the shovel.

"Okay," said Ms. Wells, sounding resigned. "I suppose it's time for us to say goodbye."

Rachael and Ms. Wells hugged cordially. Then, Ms. Wells placed a hand on Rachael's shoulder.

"Now, you have your referrals for follow-up counseling at home, right?" Rachael nodded. "And it's ninety meetings in ninety days, right?" She nodded again, less earnestly. "There are rules." She looked at Rachael, then at me. "Because they work." She gave Rachael's arm a little squeeze and then took a step back. "Well, that's it. Let me know how it's going."

"I will," Rachael said. "Thanks for everything,"

The cab driver, an old-timer with skin the color of charred leather, loaded Rachael's bag in the trunk, then held the door open so Rachael and I could slide in. We pulled away, around the circular drive and out the gate. Rachael and I looked out the back window as the building and grounds faded away.

"Bet you two aren't going to forget that place too soon," said the driver.

We turned and flopped back in the seat. "That's for sure," Rachael said.

For the rest of the drive to the airport, Rachael and I didn't say much. She rested her head on my shoulder and pressed my hand between hers. Rachael seemed lost in her thoughts.

"That was an interesting little episode of our life," I said.

"You have no idea."

"So, what's the main thing you learned?"

There was more to my question than curiosity. The Rachael I knew wouldn't be able to resist such a softball.

"Don't know where to start." Her voice was flat. "I know I'm very small and inconsequential in this big world and that there must be some kind of higher power out there. I know I'm an addict and that my addiction controls me and always will."

Was the price of sobriety going to be that I had to live the rest of my life with an AA-dogma-spouting automaton?

"The important things you learn from the other inmates. You hear their stories and you see yourself in them. Want to hear the most amazing thing?"

Not really. "Sure," I said.

"Do you know what Fentanyl is?"

"No."

"It's synthetic morphine. Just about the strongest shit out there. It's used for chronic pain management and terminal cancer patients. One way it's administered is in a time release patch you wear on your skin."

"So?" I prepared myself for a tale of how AA had rescued another lost soul from the clutches of hopeless addiction.

"I learned that if you cut open a Fentanyl patch, squeeze out the gel and lick it, it gets you high as hell."

I rested my head back on the seat, feeling the strangest combination of dread and relief.

30

The Land of No

Rachael and I were living the straight and narrow, smack in the middle of the land of no.

Two months after rehab, Rachael was seeing her therapist twice a week (the bearded Dr. Schulman, who looked like he'd been selected by central casting), putting in some hours at Big Bark, going to physical therapy for her back, eating well, and, oh yes, not doing drugs.

We found an NA meeting near our home and met many of the unfailingly nice recovering addicts who showered us with encouragement, empathy, and phone numbers. They were so friendly, so warm, so earnest as they talked recovery, drank coffee, smoked cigarettes, and talked more recovery.

Strangely enough, everyone loved, *loved*, to talk about drinking and doing drugs, especially to newbies. Invariably, someone took us aside, ostensibly to get to know us, only to regale us with stories of epic benders and lost weekends, nights spent clubbing, and running wild with the pack. The stories might have been intended as cautionary tales but, given the gleam in the eyes of the tellers, they also served to reminding us all of a time when life hadn't revolved around meetings held in dingy church basements.

We asked ourselves what good it did to hear the different versions of the same old story, told over and over again? The answer, of course, was *plenty*. Part of the process of recovery lay in the repetition, the "keep coming back," until the ritual and the stories began to take hold and make sense. Nevertheless, we began to skip meetings, then stopped going to them completely. There were certain aspects of recovery, however, that we couldn't blow off. As proof, all we needed to do was glance over at the answering machine.

Our friends had started out being supportive, offering to go to movies and shows and other "safe" activities. For the first few weeks, they were diligent about dropping by and calling us to check in. But the calls and visits had slowly tapered off. For the most part, even Rachael's rehab friends, with whom she'd felt so intimate and connected, had hit the real world, and dropped off the face of it. Arnold, the cocaine-addicted chemist, had relapsed and died of a heart attack in bed with a bag of crack and a couple of hookers, which was probably his idea of heaven.

Our sequestered life bothered me more than it did Rachael, who couldn't remember the last time she had socialized without the benefit of enhancement. "People just aren't that interesting, unless I'm high," she admitted. I, on the other hand, found the lack of social connection unbearable. My sense of connectedness and camaraderie with our friends had been one of my favorite things about our life.

About a month after Rachael's return, Trevor threw himself a party to celebrate his fortieth birthday. That night, we sat alone, trying to pretend that we would rather stay home and watch *Notorious* than be at our best friend's house only two blocks away. I could empathize with Ingrid Bergman, the bird in the gilded cage, trapped and slowly being poisoned to death by her Nazi spouse for being a double agent. Rachael cried for hours. I tried to buck her up and stay positive, but my heart wasn't in it. In fact, it was all I could do to keep a lid on my own anger and resentment. It had been Trevor, after all, who'd taken the lead in getting Rachael into rehab. Rachael's fortieth was coming up. What would we do for that, stay in and order the pupu platter?

Since Rachael had returned from rehab, my father and I had something we could talk about. He didn't mince words.

"You're in for it," he said. "Not getting high is only the beginning. You've got to be ready to change everything. What you think of as fun, where you go to find it, who goes with you. At first, the whole world feels like a trigger with the barrel pointed right between your eyes."

"How'd you get through it?"

"I jumped into the program. All the way. I almost lived in the rooms. I found a sponsor, made friends, never looked back."

"Never had a slip? Not once?"

"They don't give you a coupon for one free slip. I'm not saying it was easy. I didn't see any of my old friends for a long time. Even your grandparents weren't above offering me a little wine before dinner. Sobriety worked, but that's because I worked it. Sorry, I'm breaking out the lingo."

The night of Trevor's birthday party, however, was the first time I became aware of my resentment for the entire recovery package, including, I hated to admit, Rachael.

While Rachael had been away, I found it easy to stay away from drugs. For me, the high had never been the point. Drugs were the glue that connected me to our friends, to the tribe. I missed the banter more than the buzz. That lack of connection spilled over into all my interactions with Rachael.

Where were the unprecedented levels of closeness and communication the Tradewind's counselors said we could expect? Rachael spent most of her time at Big Bark, and the rest doing who knew what up in our office where she had set up her easel and art supplies. I descended to the basement and bashed on my drums.

She and I did experience one radical change. Sober, Rachael was insatiable. Sex became an obligation, reminding me of the way my grandmother used to demand other kinds of attention, and, believe me, having my grandmother somehow, anyhow, associated with my sex life was no aphrodisiac. Too many nights, I lay in bed hoping she'd just let me sleep.

As my father put it, "When a woman breaks your balls all day, the last thing you want is her tugging on them at night." Guilt was a strong motivator, though, and Rachael knew just how and when to apply it. I took to going through the motions, relying on porn or fantasy, often involving Trudie, to get me through. Try as I might, I just couldn't get Trudie out of my head. The contrast between my visceral craving for her and the punching-a-time-clock sex with Rachael had become even more stark. But Trudie, as everything else seemed to be, was off limits.

One night, I was splayed out across the king-sized bed in our master bedroom absent mindedly channel surfing as I waited for Chinese food to be delivered. Rachael was in the bathroom soaking in the claw-foot tub, from which I could catch an occasional whiff of jasmine and citrus scented bath salts.

I paused on Home Shopping Network to get a better look at Suzanne Sommers (not bad, considering) earnestly hawking some new exercise contraption.

The doorbell rang.

"It's General Tso," I said. "Do you want to eat him up here?"

"Yes, please."

"Okay, then, get yourself dried off."

Rachael didn't answer, but I heard water slosh in the tub and the *thunk* of the plug being pulled from the drain. Me telling Rachael what to do and her doing it. This life in recovery had turned everything topsy-turvy. I skipped down the stairs and hurried to the front door. We ordered from Blue Diamond at least three nights a week, and it was always delivered by Jorge, the nice young guy from El Salvador. I reached over to the table, grabbed the money, turned the latch, and opened the door a few inches.

There was Jorge, smiling as always.

"Twenty-seven, ninety-eight, right?"

"That's it."

I exchanged the bills for the white plastic shopping bag. "Keep the change, Jorge," I said.

"Have a good evening."

I would. A perfectly good evening, a quiet evening. A fine and uneventful motherfucker of an evening. I locked the door and walked across the length of the house to the kitchen. After arranging the food, plates, and silverware on a big, wooden tray, I strode through the empty, dark dining room, then plodded up the stairs, reminded of that first night with Rachael, that knot in my belly, feeling scared, excited, and alive.

I turned the corner into the bedroom and there was Rachael standing in front of the full-length mirror. She was naked except for a towel she had wrapped around her head like a turban. Her eyes swept up and down her own reflection.

"Food's here," I said.

Rachael turned sideways to the mirror, then three-quarters around, looking herself over. She had put on fifteen pounds in rehab and another five or so since being home. She looked healthy and strong. Her face, always her best feature, had filled out. While I'd never admit it to her, though, she was getting a little thick through the middle. Still a Caravaggio but drifting to Rubens.

"I'm fat," she said. Her voice was even and distant, with a touch of fear wedged in between.

"That's crazy," I said. "You look healthy."

"*Healthy?*" The sides of her mouth turned down sharply, "Okay, Mr. Euphemism, look at my ass and look at my stomach. I am definitely gaining weight."

"You can always drop a few pounds later."

She turned to me. "Where?"

"What I mean is I think you were *too* thin." The look on her face told me I had blown it. "Look at your tits!" I said. "What did you call them before?"

She wasn't listening. She stared at herself in the mirror, shaking her head.

"Roadkill, was it?" I asked.

"Pillowcases with curtain weights," she said, sounding distracted.

"So, come on, let's eat. What do you say?"

She stomped her foot on the floor. "It's Friday night, for Christ's sake. How many more weekends do I have to sit up here eating takeout, watching you channel surf, bored out of your mind, not saying anything? Let's call Wes."

So, this is how it happened. Our friends would be disappointed. They knew she wasn't ready, that she hadn't done nearly enough work. But they weren't the ones who had to live like this, either. I was sick of Chinese food, sick of Friday nights like these, sick of not seeing our friends. Besides, this was *her* sobriety, right? Recovery was *her* decision and *her* responsibility. That's what they said in the meetings.

I wasn't going to take the rap for this later, though, not from her and not from our friends. "I'm not making that call. Besides, you think Wes is going to allow himself to be the one that knocks you off the wagon?"

She was already headed to the phone. "He'll understand."

She was right. She would make him understand. I sat down on the bed with the tray of food on my lap. Look on the upside, I thought. From now on, plenty of leftovers.

Rachael and I spent the next several weeks proving the addiction theory which claimed that addicts will, when they relapse, pick right up where they left off. The road from cocaine and K to X and crystal was remarkably short, straight, and well paved. One Friday evening while we were up in Provincetown for a couple of weeks,

Rachael opened her hand to reveal a couple of tablets and a small baggie of white powder and that was that.

Yes, our friends were surprised and some—Trevor in particular—expressed their disappointment. There was, however, also relief on everyone's part, certainly mine. We were back.

Still, there was no getting around the fact that Rachael and I had made a pact, to get sober and stay that way for a year—a pact she had chosen to break. In my mind, that breach of contract gave me permission to do the same. As excuses go, it was pretty perfect.

One afternoon, when Rachael was at Big Bark, I drank a cocktail, did a bump, picked up the phone and placed the call I'd wanted to make for a long, long time.

.

31

A Messy Embrace

We lay in bed, me on my back, Trudie face down, her head on my chest. The sheets were twisted around us like a vine. I didn't want to know the time. I forced myself up enough to see the red readout on the motel's digital clock on the night table.

"It's almost three o'clock." I dropped my head back down to the pillow. "I've been gone a long time."

"Me too. I told the folks at the gallery I was having a gynecological procedure."

"You have this amazing way of blending the truth into your lies."

"True. If I'm gone too much longer, though, they're going to call the doctor and suggest implanting a homing device in my snatch. What did you tell Rachael?"

"Getting the car serviced."

"Again? That is one well-maintained vehicle. Want another line? There's a little bit left."

I stared at the ceiling. "No."

"A drink? There's stuff in the mini-bar."

"No."

"Something I said?"

"Nope."

"I see." She rolled off me onto her back. "So, we've come to the part of the afternoon where you begin hating yourself."

"Why would I do that? I'm only cheating on my wife with someone she thinks is a friend."

"You know it's not that simple."

"When you get right down to it, it is."

"Then why do you continue to do it?"

"It's complicated."

"Ah." She lifted one leg and scratched beneath it. "That's the most sensible thing you've said in weeks."

"Sensible? I just said I don't know why I'm sleeping with you and betraying my wife. That's not sensible, it's clueless."

"Life is messy."

"You don't need to convince me of that."

"Yeah, but to you that's something to be avoided. You need to embrace the messiness." She took a pillow and hugged it to her chest. "Learned that in therapy. Let life happen."

"If that philosophy also embraces deceit, lying, and cheating, then I've got it down cold."

Trudie swung the pillow and smacked me on the stomach. "That's not what I mean. I've been telling you since the beginning you need to come clean with Rachael, that the lies are poison. The truth will set you free, lover boy."

"Give me some credit. I resisted calling you for months."

"Until you didn't."

I took the pillow and tossed it to the floor. "Is this the part that's supposed to make me feel better about myself?"

"Sorry. You don't need any more reasons to beat yourself up. You and Rachael, you're both great at it. God, you should have seen the letters she wrote me from rehab. So hurt and angry. Especially with her father. We've all got that stuff in us, I guess. Just comes out in different ways." She crossed her arms over her head, covering her eyes. "Still," she said.

"Still what?"

"Never mind."

"Tell me."

"No. We should go."

"Say it."

Trudie paused. "Okay. I get where it comes from, but I still think someone needs to call her on the way she treats people. Especially you."

"As far as I know, she's not fucking my friend."

"I mean the way she controls you. The way she gets what she wants out of you. Right down to dressing you up like a gay boy and parading you around her friends like a Ken doll. Or one of those spoiled dogs at Big Bark."

I was reminded of how that drag queen Bianca described me as a duckling, trailing along behind its mother. I didn't like the image then and I didn't like it now. "Hey, it's not like I didn't know what I was getting into."

"You need to consider that."

"So, I'm just another recessive-gened queen."

"When I saw you on that dance floor dressed the way you were, surrounded by all those gay boys, I figured that you were, and Rachael was kidding herself. But then, the more we talked I realized I was wrong."

She dropped one hand between my legs. "And I don't mean for the obvious reasons."

"Tell me, then, why do you think I've chosen this life."

"I'm not sure you did. There's a part of you that allows someone else and what they want to choose for you. I think Rachael saw that in you, right from the get-go."

"That makes her one calculating, scary bitch."

"I don't know if she knows what she does or why she does it. When I first met her, I was bowled over. She's beautiful, smart, funny, seems to have it all together. Hell, the truth is, I had just had my heart broken by some chick. I had a crush on your wife."

"This *is* complicated."

"It took a while for me to start to see her, really see her. There's a scared little girl in there."

"Not when she's high."

"Yeah, all the drugs don't help. Scary bitch? She can be. Powerful, too. Do you realize that we spend as much time talking about her as we do having sex? More, I think."

I hadn't thought about it, but she was right. "Here's the last thing I'll say about her, then. You didn't know me before Rachael. I had no idea who I was or what I was doing or what I could do. That's different now. And it's because of her."

Trudie laughed.

"What's so funny?"

She placed her hand on my forehead. "Oh, if you could hear yourself. I used to say the same stuff when I was seeing Paul, and he was doing an eight-ball a day and beating me up. What have you found? A nice house, some

money, a Jag and getting high all the time? You think
that's going to cut it for the rest of your life? When are
you going to wake up? There is so much bottled up in
you. Somewhere along the line you shut yourself down.
And then you married someone trapped in her own little
box who'd let you stay in yours."

I grasped her hand and shoved it away. I didn't
care if Trudie was right, she had just sliced into me
pretty deeply and it was my turn to slash back. "You're
right. Let's stop talking about Rachael. Let's talk about
something we never get around to."

"Like what?"

"Like you, Dr. Phil, and how you've figured it all
out and have become so evolved as a person."

Trudie sat up and whirled toward me, her hair
spinning in a tight arc. She jabbed my shoulder with
both fists. "Don't you dare make this about me. I sit here
and listen to you go on and on about how guilty and
scared and unhappy you are, and when I suggest some
reasons you don't want to hear, you turn on me. Well,
I'll beat you to the punch. Yeah, I'm doing great. Let's
see." She counted off on her fingers. "First off, I'm doing
drugs again. Second, I'm lying to my employers who
have stuck by me like family, way better than family,
risking my whole career. Third, I've entered a dead-end
affair with a married guy who's an emotional cripple.
Should I go on? Is this helping? Because if it is, I've got
some stuff I could tell you about my father that'll make
you jump for joy." She turned her back to me, sniffed
and rubbed her nose.

I felt like I had just shoved my head into a bucket
of ice water after a three-day bender. Why had I lashed
out at Trudie of all people? "Why me? From what I hear,

the world is full of messed-up guys. Ones that aren't married to people you've slept with."

She bent over and put her head between her knees. "I don't know, exactly." The anger had left her voice. "It's not love. I don't trust you enough to love you. There's something there. But until you figure out what you want and a way to say it, you're not trustworthy. Not as a lover, not even as a friend. I don't know how many other ways I can put it."

"You can stop there."

"Until you're honest with yourself and with the people in your life, you're not ready to be with anybody."

I had never really thought of myself as autonomous, someone who could strike out on his own. I wasn't someone who made decisions by themselves and for themselves, people like Rachael who dragged the world along. I glanced over at Trudie, her pale back glowing in the dim light. No, I hadn't been that kind of person. Not until now.

Her cell phone rang. "Oh, great." She reached down and pulled it from her purse. "Hello. Yes, everything's fine. Just finished up. About an hour. See you then." She tossed the phone, which skidded and bounced across the carpeting and came to rest by the door. "Goddamn cell. Might as well be a leash."

I brought my hand up and rubbed the spot between her shoulder blades. "I'm sorry. It's been a one-way street."

Trudie took a deep breath. "Yeah, it has been one-sided, but that's my choice. Look, I may be a mess, but I am *evolved* enough to know that if you left Rachael tomorrow and begged to be with me, I wouldn't let you in. I don't need you latching on to me just because you're scared of being alone. I know what that's like. Hell, I've done it. You need to grow some as a person, Nick. If you're miserable, you've got to do something about it, for your own sake. *Before you start loving someone, you'd better start liking yourself.*" She sang the line with a country twang.

"What's that from?"

"Just made it up."

When was the last time I could remember liking myself? "How does that happen?"

"By doing the things that are right even when they're hard. Especially when they're hard."

She dropped back down next to me, her head back on my shoulder. I traced my finger around one of her dimples.

"I need to get going," I said.

"I know. One for the road?"

"Coke? No, I'm good."

"I wasn't referring to cocaine." Her hand slid down my stomach.

"I figured you'd had about enough of me."

"Of you? Maybe." She tossed her leg up and over me. "But not of this."

She leaned forward and I found her lips.

My life had gone septic. The affair with Trudie was like bandaging a wound. Not the sudden, slashing kind. This was more of an ache, a chafe, long neglected, caused by a life that was slowly wearing me down and away, erasing me, line by line.

32

Past Due

We stood in the kitchen, separated by the cooking island. "Just curious," Rachael said. "Exactly how stupid do you think I am?"

She held several sheets of paper, stapled together at the corner. She snapped the first page free from the rest and slapped it down on the countertop. Line after line of type had been carefully gone over with the broad yellow slash of a highlighter pen. She recited: "September 22, 11:14 a.m., Baltimore, Maryland 410-555-7756, fourteen minutes. September 23, 12:22 p.m., Baltimore, Maryland 410-555-7756, seventeen minutes. September 25, 4:08 p.m., nine minutes." She cleared her throat and picked up the pace. "Calls on the 27th, the 28th, the 30th." She flipped the paper over. "August 1, forty-four minutes. My, we had *lots* to talk about that day, didn't we? And my favorite, August 3. On August 3, we have four, no, sorry, *five* calls to her from your cell phone."

Rachael's lips were pulled tightly across her teeth, her jaw muscles flexed.

"Did you think that if you erased the call history from your phone, I wouldn't get suspicious? Did you think I wouldn't look at the bill? That you could continue to lie to me? That you could keep talking to her and fucking her forever."

I pictured her upstairs in the office with the bill, the desk lamp beaming down, pen in hand, carefully highlighting each listing, call after call. I had just returned from the gym and found her here in the kitchen, waiting. I didn't stand a chance. When she wanted to eviscerate, she could do it with the precision of a surgeon, like the time that contractor screwed up laying the floor in the kitchen. He was standing right where I was now when she dismantled him, tile by tile. All my life, the thought of crossing the line and having this kind of anger directed at me, vicious and retributive, had terrified me. Strangely, now that it was here, I felt far away, almost impervious. Almost.

"So, this is what you've been up to when you say you're going to the gym or getting the car fixed and don't come home for hours." She threw the rest of the papers onto the floor. "You promised me you wouldn't speak to her again." She paused. "You are not allowed to stay silent, not about this. You'd better talk to me. If you want us to stay together; you'd better start talking, and this time I want the truth."

Here was a familiar feeling, doors slamming shut, latches turning, lights out.

"Look at me," she said, positioning herself right in front of me. "This is not what adults do. I'm tired of your passive-aggressive bullshit. Talk to me."

My eyes fixated on a single sheet of paper, dangling at the edge of the countertop, raked with those yellow highlights. Even as I had made the promise not to contact Trudie again, I knew that someday I'd break it. Rachael's relapse had opened the door, so I had stood at the threshold and made a phone call. I knew it wouldn't end there. I didn't want it to. The inevitability of the outcome, the certainty of the consequences, that's what I was looking for. Like one of those serial killers who leave behind incriminating evidence, I wanted to be caught, but not because I wanted to be stopped. I wanted out.

Rachael paced back and forth, up and down the length of the kitchen, punctuating her words by driving her heels down into the floor tiles. Wherever that kitchen contractor was, I bet he just slammed his thumb with a hammer. "It's *not* the sex. Let's not forget who served her up to you on a platter. It's the lying. You said you wouldn't see her or talk to her again. Did I need to specify the cell phone? Did I need to rule out telegrams and carrier pigeons, too? By the way, don't bother calling her anymore, much less try to see her. I had a nice little conversation with Trudie. I thanked her for being *such* a friend, for lending *such* a big ear when I was in rehab. Told her the next call I'd make would be to her bosses. I'm sure they'd like to hear about her lies. I'd make sure her next job was a cashier at the carwash."

Rachael looked down at my cell phone on the countertop. "It's over." She snapped open a drawer, removed a meat tenderizer and slammed it down on the phone, shattering it into dozens of jagged splinters.

She tossed the mallet onto the counter and came up close to me. Too close.

"And so are we, if that's what you want. You can go right back to your shitty little apartment, your shitty little life, and your mother, back to delivering those lovely roses in that tuxedo. I'd like to know where else you think you'd find what we have. Look around, Nick," she said, sweeping her arm in a circle. "Who else could give you *this*. I gave you a life."

All around the kitchen were the rows of platters, vases, glassware, and china, the objects we had accumulated over the years, displayed just so. Once a month, I climbed on a step stool and dusted each one. Out beyond the picture windows was our patio, paved with vintage red bricks, each one surrounded by pale-green moss which I sprayed with a thin mist of water every week. There was the wooden fence Trevor, Wes, and I erected, lined with ceramic plant holders from Tuscany, flowers spilling out and down from them in cascades of white, pink, and orange. I had loved these things and I had cared for them. Would I miss any of it?

She took a half step closer, her face inches from mine.

"Don't you know I would do whatever it takes, anything, to protect my interests? Do you hear what I'm saying? I would do what you can't. You can't take a stand, not for us, not for me, not even for yourself." She grabbed my arm and shook it. "Speak, you fucking coward," she screamed.

The room swirled. I exploded forward, grasped her arms above her elbows and lifted. There was nothing to her. I held her above me, legs dangling down, her face a frieze of fear. I was overcome with an exquisite, exhilarating force. My lips curled back in a cruel smile. Here was the ultimate high, exultant, obliterating the gray areas, the self-doubt, the guilt. I was hot-wired. Power snapped through me like an electrical current, finding new synapses, completing circuits, resetting me. I was barely aware of standing there, holding Rachael up and away from me like an offering.

She didn't say anything. She shouldn't. Whatever kicked the door open in me was seething and looking for something, or someone, to punish. Murderous rage, the phrase ran through my head. Take three steps forward and drive her through the window. Shake her until her neck snaps. He killed her in a murderous rage, they'd say. Nice enough guy. Always said hello. My arms trembled, not from exertion, but from the certainty that I could do it.

Then, I saw her face, floating above me. Even if her intention had been to provoke me, she could not have anticipated this. That made two of us. I turned, set her down on the kitchen counter, and backed away, blinking and stunned. She rubbed her arms where I'd held her, her jaw still set hard, but her eyes gave her away. I wanted to run out the door and never stop. Dizzy and weak, I walked over to the cooking island and leaned back against it.

Her voice quivering, she said, "You need to leave here. If you don't, I'll call the police. I don't want you near this house again. Ever. I'm going to divorce you, Nick. You've made a terrible mistake that you're going to regret. That's your problem now. I'm done."

It was a good show of bravado on her part, but when I straightened up and looked her in the eyes, she shrank away.

"You're done?" I said. "We finally agree on something." I made myself form the words. "There's nothing for me here. There never was."

Before she could react, I was out of the kitchen, squeezing my hands into fists so hard they ached, liking the pain, headed for the front door, trying my best not to look at anything on the way out.

.

33

Sleep Over

When there was nowhere else to go, there was always my mother's sofa—sofa bed, to be exact. It was tan, with brushed cotton, the kind with the sadistic metal bar under the mattress that cut people right in half, left them feeling like they'd been beaten with a lead pipe, a not-so-gentle reminder that their life was a mess. Over the years, it had provided temporary refuge to more than one desperate lost soul. Once, my father had stumbled onto it, stone drunk, on what would prove to be his last binge.

Now, it was my turn.

I lay there, one leg on the floor, a glass of white wine balanced on my chest. The Valium my mother gave me beginning to work. Two days earlier, I'd shown up in a haggard daze, having walked all the way from our house following the blowout with Rachael. I hadn't been to my mother's place in months, since the time I'd swung by to pick up a couple of Percocet for Rachael who was in a bad way. I must have been quite a sight. Truth be told, I still was.

My mother poked her head out of the kitchen. "You need anything else?"

"Little more wine?"

"You're cut off."

"It worked for Judy Garland."

"Exactly." My mother emerged from the kitchen holding a juice glass half full of a thick, coffee-colored liquid.

"What's that?"

She took a seat across from me on a black leather armchair. "Kahlua."

"*You're* having a drink?"

She took a sip, sat back in the chair, and crossed her legs.

"You're tipsy," I said, amused. I had only seen her take a drink a few times in my life.

"Special occasion."

She was celebrating, something she'd never admit to but for the Kahlua.

"This is what family is all about. Don't get me wrong, I know about screwed up families. But that doesn't mean you can just write them off. That's what Rachael doesn't understand. Actually, there's a lot that girl doesn't understand." She laughed and nipped the Kahlua again.

"Better watch that stuff," I said. "Next thing you know, I'll be running you to rehab."

My mother waved me off with her free hand. "*Please.* Do you know how long that bottle has been in the cabinet? Since Larry and I went on the cruise to Mexico. It actually had dust on it."

It had been a long time since she and I sat like this. Since before Larry died. I never even made it to his funeral.

"I'm sorry," I said.

"For what?"

"For not being around."

"She didn't make it easy."

I slid back on the sofa, propped myself up against the arm, and sipped the wine. "You never really liked Rachael, did you?"

"That's not true. I tried. I just never got anything back. After a while I quit trying."

"She could be stubborn that way."

"It hurt. But that wasn't the worst part."

"What was?"

"Watching you get all caught up in her." She scratched the side of her head, just above her ear.

"What do you mean by that?"

"Your lifestyle, the money, the things. It was a trap. From the first day I met Rachael I thought that. Larry used to sit right where you are, and we'd talk about it."

"I should have seen it, but I didn't."

"You may not have wanted to see it, but you felt it. I saw it in your eyes. Just like your grandfather." She teared up. "I couldn't say any of this while you and Rachael were still together. I didn't want you to think I was being petty. I know you have plenty to think about now. Just thought it might help somehow to, you know, make some sense."

"Anyway, that's some pretty profound stuff coming from someone half in the bag on cheap coffee liquor."

"The only thing profound about me right now is my sleepiness." She slapped her thighs and stood. "I'm going to bed." She walked by me and roughed up my hair. "You'll see, everything will work out." We never hugged, which was another one of my grandmother's legacies.

"Night," I said. I downed the rest of the wine in one gulp, set it by the bed and slumped, face down, across the length of the sofa. "Now what?" I said into the mattress. Had I just replaced one catastrophe with another? Where would I live? What would I do for money? Panic and dread shoved past the Valium and wine. I reached down to the floor, dragged my hand around in circles until I found my mother's phone, leaned my head over the side of the mattress and tapped in Trudie's number. I heard the ring, tinny and distant, then the second and the third.

"Hello," she said.

I snatched the phone off the floor, almost disconnecting, and spun over onto my back. "Where the hell have you been?"

She paused. "Here."

"I must have called you ten times."

"More like twenty."

"You got my voicemails?"

"All of them."

"So?"

"How are you?"

"How do you think?"

"I knew if it happened it wouldn't be pretty."

"I need to see you."

Silence.

"Trudie?"

"I can't."

"Why not?"

"First off, I leave tomorrow for a show in London. I'll be gone for a couple of weeks. But even if I weren't the answer would still be no."

"This is no time for tough love."

"This is no time for any kind of love. I told you before." Her voice cracked. "I can't get pulled into this. I'm not doing so great myself."

"What's going on?"

"She threatened to call the owners of the gallery. I could be out on my ass. I can't handle one more thing, Nick. Especially not this."

"Maybe we could," I swallowed, "help each other."

"All we'd do is take each other down."

"Please, Trudie." I couldn't mask the desperation in my voice.

"Don't do this. You're not thinking clearly now. You need some time. We both do."

"Take all the time you need." I slammed the phone down to the floor.

34

Ninety Seconds

I leaned back in her lawyer's conference room chair and rubbed my eyes. I'd had no sleep, but I had to stay sharp. For a top divorce attorney about to negotiate a settlement for her vindictive client, Ms. Spenser wasn't the pit bull I had imagined. She'd offered me coffee, the use of the phone, even told me I could call her Mary. I could handle her. At least, that's what I kept telling myself. There was another slow, throttling constriction, like an anaconda tightening its grip around my chest and throat.

I checked my watch. It had been four minutes since Ms. Spenser left me to go fetch Rachael. My heart raced, my forehead and arm pits broke out in sweat. "Breathe," I said.

Maybe I should start counting now. No, my father was clear about how it worked. "Little trick I learned in AA," he said. "We use it to get through the cravings, but it works for anxiety too. Break time into small increments, as small as you need to get through the situation. Try ninety seconds."

Of course, I might not have needed help with the *situation* had I followed his and everyone else's advice and hired my own attorney. Apart from the money that would cost, I hadn't wanted to stir the pot, to antagonize

Rachael even more. I looked around the conference room at the good art, the plush, off-white carpeting, the conference table with the burled-walnut veneer. Who was I kidding? Ms. Spenser came off as easygoing, but you could only charge her rates and afford downtown D.C. digs like this one way. By winning.

I checked my watch again. No, I was doing this all wrong. Randomly checking the time only made things worse. It had to be ninety seconds from the time they entered the room. Then another ninety and so on, like that. I needed to think of something else, anything else.

Rachael's response to my leaving her had been swift and, in retrospect, predictable. A few days after the screaming scene in the kitchen I'd gone to make a withdrawal from an ATM. The balance in the account was zero. A call to the banking center had confirmed what I'd feared. That's when I'd had the first panic attack, standing right there on the street with nine dollars in my pocket. I took the subway back to my mother's place. Hands shaking, I called Rachael.

"Yes," she said, flat as the blade on a paring knife.

"Why is there no money in our checking account?" I pictured her tapping her chin with her index finger, smiling. "Let's see. Give me a minute. Oh, yes, I remember now. Because I withdrew it all."

"How can you possibly justify that?"

"Justify? Remember what I said to you in the kitchen before you turned into a raging maniac? That I would do whatever it took to protect my interests?"

"We're talking about a marriage here, not a corporate downsizing. That money is as much mine—"

Click.

So there I was, penniless, possibly friendless, sleeping on my mother's sofa. I needed a plan, but first I needed some cash. I got up the nerve to call Trevor.

"Man," he said, "when you do it, you do it big."

"You heard," I said, disappointed. I'd wanted to tell him my version of things, my way.

"I've heard. So has everybody but Oprah."

"Let me guess. I come off pretty bad."

"There's you, Jeffrey Dahmer, Stalin and some guy whose name I can't remember who impaled babies on stakes."

"You left out Hitler."

"No. I didn't. Unlike you, Hitler had some redeeming qualities. He liked dogs."

I was about to insist I liked dogs, too, until I realized I was about to make the case to my friend that I possessed redemptive qualities equal to those of Hitler.

"Listen," said Trevor, "even I wouldn't joke with you if I thought half of what she told me was true. I know how it's been. You okay? How you fixed for money?"

At that moment if Trevor had asked me to marry him, I'd have gone straight out shopping for a trousseau. I borrowed a few thousand dollars, enough to live on until we reached a settlement, but not enough, I told myself, to hire an attorney.

"Are you crazy," my father said. "That's like boxing with one hand tied behind your back, like dancing with one leg, like showing up to a gunfight with a knife—"

"Enough with the similes. I got it," I said.

"Well if you *got* it, why don't you go out and hire yourself an attorney?"

"I can handle her," I said. "That's why." So, instead of seeking counsel, I sat down and wrote Ms. Spenser a series of carefully constructed letters, laying out in the most logical and reasonable terms my proposal for a fair and equitable division of our assets. I had not received a response.

The door to the conference room swung open and they entered, Ms. Spenser in the lead, brisk and business like, Rachael just behind her, jaw set, wearing a black Chanel suit and holding a Vuitton briefcase. Dressed to annihilate. Throw in some flashing lights, a deep voiced announcer, a rabid crowd, and you had the start of an Ultimate Death Match.

My throat tightened. Five seconds.

The two women sat side by side, opened their briefcases and began removing file after file, stacking them next to each other like fastidious waiters setting an elegant table. Rachael's perfume, something I hadn't smelled before, slammed me like a floral-infused fist.

Fifteen seconds.

Rachael wouldn't look at me, intent on arranging her files just so. When she finished, she closed the briefcase clasp with a surprisingly loud *snap*. She placed the briefcase beside her, put her hands on the table, interlocked her fingers and glared at me, unblinking.

My scalp was on fire, thousands of follicles begging for relief, but I didn't dare give in. I didn't dare move anything but my gaze, down to my watch.

Forty seconds.

Ms. Spenser adjusted her reading glasses, cleared her throat and said, "We all know why we're here, so let's get down to business. We've received your correspondence regarding the terms of your settlement and have found it completely unacceptable." She slid a file folder across the table at me. It stopped two inches from my right hand, which I was pressing down so hard onto the gleaming table top I was sure it would leave a divot.

Fifty seconds.

"We've prepared an alternative arrangement which we believe is much more realistic." Another folder skidded toward me, this one launched by Rachael. It rested next to the first, forming a perfect L.

I willed my left hand to open the file. "Assets" was written across the top, a trail of numbers cascaded down. I shifted my eyes from the paper to my watch and left them there.

Seventy seconds.

Ms. Spenser said, "As you'll see, we've proposed that the settlement take into account the considerable mental anguish—"

"Excuse me," I said.

Ms. Spenser looked at me over the top of her reading glasses.

"Yes?"

"I have to use the bathroom."

They gave each other sidelong glances. "Just past the reception area," Ms. Spenser said.

"Thank you," I said. I stood and walked out of the room, springing along the thickly padded carpeting past the pretty receptionist with the tiny hands. She was on the phone.

"Bathroom?" I mouthed to her, pointing straight ahead. She smiled and nodded. Past the men's room I found what I was looking for, an exit door, which I plowed through, freefalling down the steps two at a time. Four flights down and I burst into the pale, marble-lined lobby and out the revolving door into the bustle of K

Street. I leaned against the building, closed my eyes, threw my head back and took in a lungful of crisp, autumn air.

I walked to the corner to hail a cab. As I did, I did the math: ninety seconds before they wondered what was up. Ninety more until Ms. Spenser asked the receptionist about me. Another ninety until they put it together.

A yellow cab pulled up. I reached out to open the door and the face of my watch glinted in the sun. I smiled. Had to tell my father he was right, about everything. Turns out ninety seconds was plenty of time. All you ever needed.

35

Come On, Get Happy

It would be a stretch to call my impromptu Houdini impersonation at the attorney's office a strategy. My decision to flee had involved the same planning and foresight as yanking my hand out of a vat of boiling oil. Though it wasn't my proudest moment, the episode did lead to one unintended consequence that turned out to work in my favor. Like a couple of used car salesmen who were sure they had the customer just where they wanted him only to have him bolt from the showroom, my disappearing act made it obvious to Ms. Spenser and Rachael that they needed to hammer out a deal. Fast.

According to Washington, D.C. divorce law, I was entitled to half of everything Rachael and I had accumulated while we were together, which was everything. Unless Rachael wanted to risk liquidating every single thing she owned, she needed to present me with a revised counteroffer before I had time to reconsider and get lawyered-up. The day after our truncated meeting, a polite and subdued Ms. Spenser called to tell me she'd have something for me to look over in a few days.

In the end, Rachael ended up with the house, the business, and the car. I received the cash in our checking and savings account, which totaled about fifty thousand dollars. As numbers on a spreadsheet, the settlement was far from equitable. The value of the assets she got were many, many times fifty thousand dollars. But I wasn't looking for equitable. I was looking for a new start, with enough cash to buy me some time.

Now what?

Trevor and Wes suggested I visit them in Provincetown, where they'd rented a house for the month of July. At first, I resisted. Provincetown burst with memories of times when things were fresh and new and exciting. There was no denying the fact that I needed a break from the drama, not to mention my mother's sofa. Was I ready for Provincetown, though, a place in which I'd never stepped foot without Rachael?

"Come on," Wes said. "You could use a little fun."

"Where would I stay?"

"With us. We'll make it all about you."

"But I—"

"Not I. *You.*"

"Well—"

"Great. We'll see you this weekend."

I caught the shuttle up to Boston and took the mid-day ferry. I decided to walk from the docks through the center of town, past shirtless muscle-boys; couples (gay and straight) pushing babies in strollers; skateboard punks; mullet-haired dykes in sleeveless shirts; Harley riders in fringed-leather jackets; fawn-like teenage girls wearing too-tight low-rise jeans; drag queens and comedians hawking their shows; and old folks wearing comfortable shoes. Drivers dumb enough to try to navigate their SUVs down jam-packed Commercial Street crept right along with the pedestrians and bicycle riders. Outside of town hall, Ellie, the swinging seventy-two-year-old transsexual, wearing her signature denim mini-skirt and four-inch heels, belted out "Get Happy" into a mic attached to a portable karaoke machine she hauled around in a little red wagon.

Nice gams, I thought.

There was a friendly, familiar buzz to the town that fit me like a pair of well-worn jeans.

Trevor, Wes, and I spent the rest of that afternoon up on the deck of their house, set up high in the dunes with a sweeping view of the Provincetown harbor, and beyond that, the brilliant blue of the sailboat-specked bay. We sipped cocktails and avoided talking about Rachael.

Wes had finally come to terms with his hair via a pair of clippers. I spun him around. "I'd have said you were crazy, but bald kind of works for you," I said.

"Thanks for the ringing endorsement."

"I like it." I rubbed my hand back and forth over his shaved head. "Just takes some getting used to." I pointed to the base of his skull which formed a distinct V. "What's the significance of this?"

"I haven't decided. It's either *V* for 'very hot guy' or an arrow pointing straight to my ass."

"As if there's anyone left on the planet that doesn't know where your ass is," Trevor said.

"Sometimes I think you've forgotten."

"The more I look at it, the more it grows on me," I said.

"My ass or my head?" said Wes.

"Tell me again, which is which?" said Trevor.

I laughed.

"See," said Wes, pinching my cheek, "there's a smile. You should listen to your uncle Wes more often. You stay here as long as you like. There's only one rule this weekend. We have fun. Like the old days."

"I'll try." I took a big breath. "Have you heard from her?"

"What do *you* think?" Trevor said.

"How is she?"

"Pissed."

"Does she know I'm here."

"That's why she's pissed," said Wes.

"I hate putting you two in the middle of this."

Trevor stroked his mustache. "I've known Rachael for a long time. I will always love that girl. But she can be a raging cunt. We both can. In fact, it's the foundation of our friendship. She needs to understand that she had something to do with what happened between you. So do you."

"That doesn't mean that by seeing you we are betraying her," Wes said.

That is exactly how it would seem to Rachael.

Sleepy from the trip and the alcohol, I dozed off and woke at sunset to find a note on the dining room table. "Off to the Crown—*be there*." I put on my torn jeans and a tank top and shot out the door.

"Aren't you Nick of Rachael and Nick?" asked the perky, curly haired boy sitting at the table outside the entrance of the Crown & Anchor.

"Used to be," I replied. "I mean, it used to be Rachael and Nick."

"How exciting," he said. "Feels like I'm talking to a celebrity." I didn't quite know what to say to that, so I didn't say anything. He fidgeted with the green glow-in-the-dark band around his neck. His demeanor shifted to sympathetic and solemn. "I'm *so* sorry. I heard."

Who hadn't heard? The word of our break-up had spread quickly, like the shock wave from a nuclear explosion, first among our closest circle of friends, then the supporting players, acquaintances, and now, apparently, twenty-two-year-olds working the door at the Crown & Anchor.

"You doing okay?" he asked.

"Uh, yeah." I looked past him to the entrance to the club, feeling anxious. "Meeting my friends inside."

He nodded earnestly. "Oh, that's *such* a great idea. It really helps to have your friends around you. I know, I've been there." As we spoke few people lined up behind me. "When Barry and I split, I thought my life was over."

I could feel eyes burning a hole through my back. "I should get in there," I said.

"He checked his watch. "Goodness, you're right." He slid the admission strap across the table. "You have yourself a good time, honey." Softly, so the others behind me couldn't hear, he added, "The cover's on me. We brokenhearted have to stick together."

I approached the entrance to the club, which throbbed with music, held up my left wrist to the doorman and stepped inside. Dense, humid air shrouded me. I stood on the edge of the dance floor, letting my eyes adjust to the lights. Already, I was sweating. I took off my shirt, tucked it in my jeans and headed to the nearest bar for water. Rumor had it that on the busiest nights, the owner of the Crown turned off the cold water to the bathroom sinks to force bottled water sales. It was an effective business strategy, I decided, as I paid my four dollars.

I needed to find Trevor and Wes. I slid into the crowd and turned a full circle looking for a familiar face, instead found myself surrounded by an endless tangle of shoulders, arms, and shaved heads. Holding my bottle of water above my head like a torch in a cave, I made my way to the spot we always used to congregate, just under a series of platforms set against the wall like bleachers.

I was almost to the corner when I spotted the back of Wes's head and that distinctive V. I grabbed Wes's shoulders with both hands and squeezed hard. The physical connection felt grounding and familiar. He had his arms draped around someone's waist. It wasn't Trevor. Wes craned his head back over his neck. Finally, he recognized me and smiled, took one hand off the boy's waist and grabbed me around the neck, pulled me to him and planted a kiss on my forehead. His body glistened with sweat. Wes yelled something. I caught every other syllable, like a defective speaker at the drive-through. I shook my head. "What?"

"'turd – na – val – eez!" he said, laughing, like a stand-up comic doing his routine in Kurdish.

I gave up on conversation. I put my mouth right to his ear and shouted, "Trevor?"

He shrugged. Wes tapped the shoulder of his dance partner, a short guy whose pupils drifted along like sleeping fish in an aquarium, and tried, in vain, to make introductions. Wes and he turned their backs to me and continued their dance. I swayed in place as sweat ran down my face, the back of my neck, my arms, my chest, soaking the top of my jeans. I drained the water, now lukewarm, in one long swig. I spotted a small space that had opened up behind me on the first tier of the bleachers set against the wall. I hopped onto it. From my perch, I saw a few familiar, blissed-out faces dancing to yet another screeching-diva anthem, followed next by a ridiculous remix of the theme song to *The Price Is Right*.

No air, bad music, no drugs, no friends—no wife. I caught myself in mid-wallow. Still, the so-familiar setting combined with my lack of connection to it juked me. How many times had I danced in this very spot, on this stupid bleacher, feeling on top of the world? The faces were all around me, the lights playing off their features. Desperation. Chasing the tail of the dragon. The next night, strike the set, move on to the next town and do it all over again. How had I not seen it before? Because I'd thought I was above it, because I was straight, because I was with Rachael. But here, alone, I was just another one of the boys. Trevor was right. I was out of my league. What he left out is that we all were. Strip away the glitter and what were we? A bunch of minor-leaguers, pretending to be in the show. I had done what I said I would and out-gayed the gays. What had it gotten me? I stood with my feet planted squarely in two worlds, not belonging in either. It was time to take those big-ass strides Bianca had suggested, right on out of here I leapt down off the bleachers and slipped on the wet floor. To steady myself, I grabbed the shoulder of a brawny guy who glanced at me, annoyed, before turning away. I worked my way across the club, towards the exit. Almost there, I saw a familiar face. I had no idea who he was or where we'd met. He smiled at me, then squinted, trying to place me. Without Rachael I was out of context.

Nearly to the door, I felt a hand on the back of my neck. I turned. It was Trevor.

"Where you going?" he asked.

"Good question."

Trevor studied my face like he was trying to make sense of a puzzle. He motioned towards the back of the club. "Outside."

I followed him out through the back doors leading to the pool and deck, set against the harbor. Our skin steamed in the cool air. We wound our way through the crowd, stopping once to say hello to a few acquaintances, who treated me with the strained, sugary concern usually reserved for newly diagnosed cancer patients. Finally, we got drinks at the thatched tiki bar and found a couple of empty seats at a table over in the far corner of the deck. A new moon shown over the harbor, bright, fresh, and full. The masts of sailboats wagged in the moonlight.

Trevor took a swig from his Cape Codder and leaned back in his chair. "What's going on?"

"Sure you want to know? I thought it was all fun and games this weekend."

"It was until I got a look at you. Last time I saw that expression on a guy's face, I was at his funeral."

I took a swallow of water. "I thought it would be different. Like the old days, right? But it's not. I went ahead and blew up my life. For what? Rachael and I had our problems, sure, but at least I knew where I stood. We had friends." I pointed to the people milling around on the pool. "We had this."

Trevor took his free hand and rubbed it back over his hair. "I've done two hits of pretty good X and several cocktails. The reason I mention it is I'm about to get serious, and I need you to pay close attention because I don't know how long I can maintain. Okay?"

I nodded.

"I never told you this before, but when I first met you, I resented the hell out of you."

"You made that pretty clear."

"Know why?"

"You said I was playing out of my league."

"Want to know what I meant?"

I nodded.

"I thought, here's this straight guy with the beautiful wife that gets all the benefits of this life without having to pay any dues." He paused. "This is where you're supposed to ask me 'What dues?'"

"Since when do you need a prompt?"

"Like growing up knowing you're different from everybody else, thinking you're the only freak in the world. Laugh along with the faggot jokes at school, hating yourself the whole time. Kiss some guy in a bathroom stall and feel so ashamed the next day, all you can think about is how you'll word the suicide note. Stay up night after night, your guts a mess, because you know if you get up the nerve to tell your parents you're a faggot, there's a good chance your father, the man you admire most in the whole fucking word, will never speak to you again. Wonder if you're going to die because the condom slipped. Understand?"

I didn't answer. I couldn't.

"So, you get through all that. You carve out a life for yourself. Meet someone you'll know you'll be with the rest of your life. Make some money. Tell yourself you don't have to give a shit anymore what anybody thinks about you. You create this club, the circuit, which is like a big 'fuck you' to the world. Where everyone understands you, where everybody's fabulous. And then, after all that pain, all that work, all those dues, in strolls this straight dude, ambles up to the bar like he owns the place. Get it?"

I flushed from anger. "Yeah. You think I'm an arrogant asshole."

"You are confusing yourself with me." Trevor put

his hand on my shoulder. "That's how I felt at first. But then, I got to know you better, and I understood something. That you were as confused and lost as I used to be. What I get about you is that you've never lived your life for yourself, always through other people, for other people. Leaving Rachael?" He took his hand off my shoulder and put it on my cheek, "That's your coming out. And nothing is free. I learned that in business, and I learned it in life. All this you're feeling? They're your dues. With interest accrued."

I took a long swig from my cocktail and looked up to the moon. "I'm banished. Is that what you're trying to tell me?"

"Leave the melodrama to the fags. We're so much better at it." Trevor sighed, then smiled. "What I'm saying is it's a big world. Go out and find where you belong. That was never going to happen for you, not with Rachael. Don't waste your time trying to recreate what you had. The whole point is not to. Besides, this?" He motioned to the crowd. "This isn't a life. It's a party."

All this time I thought Trevor had meant I wasn't good enough to be gay, when what he was really trying to tell me was that trying to be gay was never going to be good enough for me. Something had just ended or just begun. Maybe it was both. I leaned forward and we touched, forehead to forehead.

He reared back and said, "Right. Now, I'm going to spend the rest of the evening trying to reenact several of the most degenerate scenes from *Caligula*. What are your plans?"

"I'm out of here."

"I bet there's some drunken snatch over at the Governor Bradford with your name on it."

"You, my friend, are one tawdry-assed sissy."

We plowed back through the crowd and parted at the dance floor. I made my way out the way I had come in, past the same kid working the door.

"*Hey*," he said, "done so soon?"

I stopped to put on my shirt. "I am. Thanks again for the comp."

"Oh, sure. Least I could do." He checked his watch. "Almost midnight. Where to?"

I looked both ways down Commercial Street. There was nothing but dark store fronts and a few early birds sitting on the steps in front of Spiritus Pizza, nibbling on slices, waiting for the throngs to join them after the clubs closed. I shrugged. "Good question."

He shook, as though a chill had just run through him. "Don't you just love the night. So full of possibilities."

I smiled. "One way to look at it."

36

Tête-à-Tête, Mano-a-Mano

My impromptu July 4th visit to Provincetown had, at Trevor and Wes's urging, stretched into a short sabbatical. Far away from Rachael and her attorney, not to mention my mother's sofa, that summer in Provincetown wrapped itself around me like a cloak of mink.

The days were filled with bike rides to the end of Bradford Street and the path leading to the boy beach, enduring Trevor's verbal jabs at my bike, a retro beach cruiser with white-wall tires and the basket festooned with Mardi Gras beads, dubbed the gayest bike in Provincetown. Trevor, Wes, and I would slosh across the marshy wetlands in thigh-deep water, climb over the dunes down to the shore, smoke a joint and watch the boys cruise us. As Trevor and Wes rated the passing parade of cocks and asses, I watched them flirt in that easy, direct way that always made flirting between straight people seem so awkward and forced.

Evenings were often spent cooking in and eating out on the deck. Friends came over regularly, some close, some merely acquaintances. To my surprise, probably theirs too, I had plenty to talk about. People told me they felt they were getting to know me for the first time.

That is precisely how I began to feel about the world. I was seeing it with brand new eyes. Mine. I did what I wanted when I wanted, including things Rachael wouldn't do, such as karaoke night at the local dive, the Governor Bradford, or dancing to Space Pussy, a metal band with a transsexual drummer who performed in a striped bikini. My friend, Roxanne, the percussionist with Mannheim Steamroller, had me join her to play conga drums over the house music at the Crown & Anchor and the crowd loved it.

One evening during the Friday night gallery crawl, I met a young blonde who worked at a restaurant on the east end of town. She took me sailing by day and barhopping at night. It turned out that, in a town known worldwide for its gayness, there was a thriving straight scene with its more-than-occasional opportunities for hetero debauchery.

On a lark, I signed on for a workshop at the Fine Arts Work Center, submitted a story about my grandmother for critique. The instructor took me aside and told me to keep at it. I was good. I couldn't remember the last time someone had said that to me.

Then, Trevor broke the news to me that Rachael was in town for a week of vacation. My instinct was immediate and overpowering. To flee.

"You gave her almost everything," he said. You going to hand her Provincetown, too?"

"For a week, she can have it," I said, "Otherwise I'm walking around town like a spooked cat, just waiting to turn a corner on Commercial Street and *bam*."

"That's exactly why you need to face her. Wes and I aren't the only ones who feel this way."

"Who else?"

"About this tall." he said, indicating the top of his chest, "Dimples, tattoos, pierced nipples, nice ass?"

"Trudie?"

"She called me to find out how you're doing."

I had been thinking about Trudie, almost picked up the phone to call her several times. But I had fought off the urge. My ego wasn't quite up for abject rejection. Besides, as much as I hadn't wanted to hear it, her mistrust of me and my intentions were justified. I wasn't ready. Closer, maybe, but not there.

"What did you tell her?" I asked.

"The truth. Had any panic attacks?"

"Not for a long time."

"And there's the writing, the, um, socializing with that trollop. I see a change. I see *you*. It's time. For your sake and hers. Not to mention mine and Wes's."

That's when he proposed a meeting, somewhere neutral, somewhere where we'd both be comfortable, like warring heads of state or rival mob bosses. I agreed. In principle, at least.

"You give me a time and place," I said, confident it would never happen, "and I'll be there."

"Wes and I are having lunch with her today. I'll try to set something up."

Truth was, I wanted Rachael to nix the meeting. I'd be off the hook and could feel morally superior, having made the grand gesture. For the moment at least, I could let my guard down. I felt safe up here at Trevor and Wes's, glad to have the place all to myself on this sparkling day. I put in a load of laundry, took a long, cool outdoor shower, and let the late summer sun dry me off and drain the tension out of me. I was outside on the deck, naked, sipping an iced tea, sitting on one of the generously padded Pottery Barn lounge chairs, bossa nova slinking from the outdoor speakers, leisurely folding my first load of laundry still warm from the dryer, feeling drowsy and a little decadent.

Then, my phone rang.

I sauntered across the broad gray expanse of the deck towards the wrought iron table where I had left the phone. Surrounding the deck, the wildflower garden Wes planted had recently burst to full bloom. A tall, violet, butterfly bush had attracted several monarchs, angling and swooping in every direction, the contrasting ribbons of color in their wings enhanced by the unfiltered sun.

I looked at the caller ID. It was Trevor, probably calling to tell me Rachael had put the kibosh on the meeting. I was prepared to sound indignant but feel relieved. I snapped open the phone.

"How was lunch?" I asked.

"Where are you?"

"At your house."

"Listen, I don't have much time. She's in the bathroom. The meeting's on."

I managed a weak, unconvincing, "Good. When?"

"How about now?"

"Now? As in *now* now?"

A few feet away, a butterfly landed on a blossom. Just a moment ago, it had been exquisite. Now, its wings pulsed methodically, diabolically, like a bellows, creating a tiny wisp of wind that would, no doubt, weeks from now and thousands of miles away, burst into a devastating, ravaging storm. Lives would be lost.

"We need to seize the moment. How about I bring her over? You guys chat for a while out on the deck, then I'll run her back to town."

I looked down. My balls were nowhere in sight. I envied them. "Well, I just don't know. I mean, I'm in the middle of doing laundry."

Trevor was silent. He had taken the initiative and gone through the trouble to set this whole thing up and I was trying to get out of it, because my socks and underwear were in the rinse cycle.

"How long until you get here?" I asked.

"About twenty minutes."

"Uh, Trevor?" I said, trying too hard to be casual. "Valium."

Trevor stifled a laugh. "In the master bedroom. The drawer on the left side of the bed. They're ten milligrams, so break one in half. Don't take the whole thing or we'll find you passed out on the deck."

That sounded okay to me.

By the time I flipped the phone shut, I was already through the screen door and halfway up the steps to the master bedroom. I took the steps two at a time to the top level, turned the sharp corner into the master bedroom, hit the area rug, and slid over to the bed. I found the bottle of Valium where Trevor said it would be, popped open the lid, bit a pill in half, and swallowed it down. Next, down to the kitchen, where I opened the freezer, yanked out the vodka and poured myself a stiff cocktail with just a splash of cranberry juice. I took a long, deep pull from the drink as I headed back out to the deck, my mind still racing.

There I stood, pacing around in little circles, cocktail in hand, waiting for my buzz, and my ex, to arrive. In that order, I hoped. How was it that someone who was supposed to be irrelevant still had the power to make me chase my tail around in circles? The answer to that would have to wait. Just then, I needed to figure out how to play it. Two scenarios came to mind:

I was dressed in silk pajamas like Cary Grant, sprawled on the lounge chair reading the New Yorker. *I rose to kiss the back of her hand. "Well, hello, darling," I said. "How in the world have you been? Can I get you a cocktail? I think we should dispense with all this silly bitterness, don't you? Time we were civilized and adult about things." I removed two Dunhills from my engraved sterling case, put them both in my mouth, lit them, and slid one between her lips. We discussed world events and fashion as we sipped martinis from crystal stemware.*

Cool was risky. What if she saw right through it? Maybe white hot was the better move:

I leaned against the wrought iron table, wearing torn jeans, a tight white T-shirt with the sleeves cut off, arms crossed and silent, sizing her up as she approached me. I was James Dean. No, better yet, Brando. I was an animal presence, a coiled spring, unpredictable. I hadn't bathed for days. Scrape away the cool and I seethed. Don't fuck with me, bitch; there's just no telling what I may do.

An ice-cold drop of condensation fell from the bottom of my glass onto my big toe. I looked down at my foot and realized I was standing in the middle of the deck stark naked. Here I was deciding on which persona to wear, and I hadn't bothered to put on any clothes. For the briefest moment, I thought about greeting her just like that, smiling, hands on my hips like an underwear model from the old Sears catalog, minus the underwear.

I walked over to the lounge chair, piled high with my folded laundry, rummaged through it and came up with jeans and a navy-blue Provincetown T-shirt. That would have to do. I hurried to pull them on. I gathered up the laundry, slid the screen door open with my elbow and headed down to the guest room, leaving a trail of socks and underwear in my wake. I dumped the laundry onto the bed, went to the bathroom and combed my hair, regarding myself in the mirror. I was tanned and had been hitting the gym regularly. How would she think I looked? *Wait a minute.* I tossed the comb onto the vanity. Why should I care? Trevor was right. I was doing better. Why would I let *her* creep back inside and muck things up?

My father had a theory. "As bad as she was for you," he said, "she's familiar, too, right? It's like me and booze. I know it would take me down hard and fast. But there's still a little part of me that misses it. You've got to recognize that. Otherwise, she'll blindside you. And that wouldn't be pretty."

There was the sound of car tires grinding against gravel. I retraced my steps back to the deck, pausing to collect the laundry I had dropped which I rolled into a ball and dumped onto a lounge chair. Trevor's silver Mercedes pulled into the driveway. The sun reflected hard off the windshield. I remembered my cocktail, sitting where I left it on the deck. I reached down and took one more swallow.

There she was, an apparition, a mirage. If she were a hologram, I would have said whoever programmed her had gotten it just about right. The measured walk; the smile, broad and wry; brilliant white teeth; makeup and bright-red lipstick expertly applied; jewelry everywhere. But a few things were slightly off: her hair, which was shorter now, more styled, the color redder than I remember. And her clothes: tight, low-rise jeans, the kind I could never get her to wear. A pale-blue halter top, barely containing her breasts. Bright blue, pointy-toed boots made of lizard or snakeskin—a little flashy, especially for this time of day. I wasn't the only one who'd put some thought into their costume and their persona.

She was just a few feet away, and I stood, arms open. As Trevor and Wes passed, Wes said, "We'll be inside." His expression told me to scream if I needed anything.

Rachael's body pressed against mine. I was overcome by the familiar scent of jasmine. I squeezed her close, then remembered her bad back and let up a little. The anxiety left me, as did the desire to engage in any kind of emotional chess match.

Then, a thing happened I didn't expect. Something deep inside me gave way. I began to cry. Huge rolling, bursting sobs poured from me. Once it began, I couldn't stop. I was so overwhelmed by the surge, I couldn't identify the source. It wasn't fear, or regret, shame, or guilt, all the usual suspects. My body convulsed and heaved. I squeezed her tighter and she squeezed back, though not with the same conviction. We stood like this for a while.

"I'm so sorry," I managed to say, half laughing, considering the stupendous irony. Only now that we were apart could I display the vulnerability she wanted from me. Rachael was going through the motions of consoling me, but she wasn't crying. In the tentativeness of her embrace, I felt she didn't know quite what to make of me. Neither did I. I dragged the back of my hand across my eyes, smearing tears across my face. "I've turned into a blubbering idiot."

"You know, not once in ten years did I ever see you cry."

She was right. I never let my guard down like this. Not ever. Not when my grandparents died, not in the black times after Fire Island. "I suppose I'm making up for lost time." I took a step back from her. She looked me over.

"You look great," she said. "Still missing the aging gene."

"You know me." I blinked my eyes to clear them, the crying over, at least for now. "I'm Dorian Gray. Somewhere in a closet there's a portrait of me that looks like Freddy Krueger."

"Let's sit," she said.

The vodka, Valium, and crying had drained me, but I also hadn't felt so calm and relaxed in months, maybe years. We sat across from each other at the table. I watched Rachael fish a pack of cigarettes and a lighter out of her small black purse and go through the motions of lighting it.

"You started smoking again?" I said.

"Like a fiend," she said, exhaling. I braced myself for the sickening smell of cigarette smoke, but this was different. It was pungent but sweet, like incense.

"What is that?" I said.

"Clove. They're terrible for you, so I love them."

"Can I try one?"

"You smoke now?"

"No."

"Help yourself." She slid the pack across the table.

I pulled one out, stuck it between my lips and lit it. I rolled the cigarette between my index and middle fingers, watching the smoke drift upward. What an excellent prop a cigarette is. "So," I said, "how are you?"

She gave a cautious little smile. "Better."

"I'm glad we did this. It was going to be a rough week, otherwise."

"I know," she said, waving her cigarette. "It was time, I suppose."

I wasn't getting hostility from her. It was more like detachment, as if she was reading from a script she hadn't had enough time to memorize.

"How is Big Bark?"

"Doing fine. Plenty of competitors now."

"That figures. You were right about that business, though. It was the next big thing."

"Big things come; big things go."

I let that one pass. "Anna still there?"

"Yes, thank goodness. She kept the whole place running. I was in pretty bad shape there for a while. Didn't get out of bed for weeks."

The guilt card. "How is your back?"

She shrugged. "Good days and bad days. Mostly bad. The doctors suggest surgery, but I'm not quite ready for that."

"Must be tough."

She nodded dismissively. "It has given me another idea for a business, though."

"What's that?"

"Gay retirement communities."

I laughed.

"No, really. Think about it. Where are they going to go, once the party's over. Most of them without kids, without families, estranged, disowned, whatever? They've got some money and they don't want to be alone. Now they don't have to be. They get peace and quiet, tasteful décor, and the company of other fags."

She had constructed a whole business model around her personal profile. Brilliant.

"In the next ten years, millions of them will be retiring. I'm telling you, it's the next big thing."

"I'm sure it is. Have a name yet?"

She smiled. "I was thinking EKG Acres."

I laughed. "Perfect," I said. "All those old circuit queens cooking down the Ensure and snorting it."

"Glow in the dark dentures."

"Deejays in wheelchairs."

"Earl Grey Tea dances."

"Versace-designed hospital gowns."

Riffing with Rachael. It was like riding a bicycle. "Well," I said, "you'll have to save a bed for me."

She almost smiled. "And you?"

"I'm thinking Miami."

She nodded approvingly. "Why not? Nice weather, the beach. Hot girls."

"Seems like a place to start over."

"What are you going to do?"

"I have no earthly idea. I've started writing, though."

"Writing?"

"Stories. I like it."

She looked momentarily surprised, then pleased, as if she had just figured something out. "I bet you're good at it. You always were a good observer."

For the briefest second, just as I had during dinner at that Ethiopian restaurant a million years earlier, I felt the spellbinding power of her affirmation. The thing I admired most about Rachael was her certainty that anything was possible.

"Seeing anyone?" she asked.

It was her way of asking me about Trudie. "No."

She seemed relieved. "You should try the Internet. With that tan and long hair, you'd get a million hits."

"Seems kind of impersonal," I said.

"Are you kidding? As bad as we are at flirting, impersonal is an advantage. You cut through all the bullshit and get right down to business."

She had a point. We'd always said our flirting repertoire consisted of not making eye contact and staring at our feet.

"After you left, I went crazy on these dating sites. It's a brave new world out there. No shortage of younger guys looking for older women. I went through tons of them. Never had so much sex in my life."

I hadn't known what to expect from this meeting, but it wasn't this. I knew she was giving me a blast of not-so-passive aggression, but her casual delivery was throwing me, acting as though she was catching up with one of her gay buddies instead of the man she was married to for ten years.

"Only a couple stuck for more than a night or two. But one of them really helped me discover myself sexually." She took another drag from her cigarette and, not knowing how to respond, I did the same. "Not the most stable guy in the world. Kind of a mess, actually. But he introduced me to the whole fetish scene."

"Fetish?"

"You know, dominance and submission and role playing. I found out I can be quite the little submissive."

Rachael, a submissive?

"Apparently, the more controlling you are outside the bedroom, the more you want someone to tell you what to do in bed. Anyway, I got heavy into that scene. Remember the closet leading from the bedroom to the bathroom?"

"Yeah."

"Now it's full of restraints, schoolgirl outfits, and naughty-nurse uniforms."

The surreal quality of this meeting was sinking in. Here was a cardboard cut-out of Rachael sitting across from me, describing yet another extreme lifestyle as she recounted her sexual exploits. Was this the person I was with for all those years? There was no jealousy in me, not even a pang. Sex had never been the primary connection between us, anyway. I wanted like to make up some outrageous sexual escapade to counter hers, though, something about a van full of strippers. But the moment had passed. Besides, there was something much more important I needed to say to her.

I crushed the nearly spent cigarette against the glass tabletop and dumped the butt in my empty glass. "That day in the kitchen? I know I scared you. Scared myself, too. I should never have let it get to that point. I'm sorry about that."

Rachael took a puff and let it out. "Yeah, well, we were pushing each other pretty hard, weren't we? For a long time."

That was as close to either forgiveness or an apology as I was ever going to get. "Mind if I have another one of those cigarettes?" I said.

"Sure," she said, handing me one. "Delicious, aren't they?"

I nodded yes, reached over for the lighter. "You have to excuse me if I seem a little off, but I was so damn nervous about this meeting, I slammed down a whole Judy Garland cocktail."

"Really. I'd never have known."

"That's adrenaline for you."

I lit the cigarette. As I did, I tried to think of another topic of conversation that didn't involve sex and fetishes.

"Speaking of adrenaline." I would never have brought it up if I thought she was high, but she looked healthy and calm.

"Crystal?" she asked. " Under control. But wow, I finally get that crystal-sex connection."

So much for changing the subject.

"After you left, I hit it hard, but I'm staying away. I have a tough enough time getting out of bed without being suicidal. Besides, all I need to do is look around at some of our friends to see what can happen if you give in to it. Have you heard from Hector?"

Hector was, not surprisingly, part of the group of friends who'd drifted her way following our breakup. "No."

"He had to leave the clinic, give up his practice, everything. He's in rehab in Ft. Lauderdale right now. And none of this twenty-eight-day bullshit. I'm talking three-month rehab for doctors."

So, Trevor had been right all along about Hector.

"And you?" she asked.

"I've been out to the clubs a few times, but it's not the same. The parties, the scene, the drugs. It all feels like it's trying too hard. High just isn't all it's cracked up to be anymore."

She laughed. "Yeah, well, what is? Twilo is shut. They sold Palladium to NYU and turned it into dorms."

"Beware the yuppie scum," I said.

"Got that one right." Rachael stood, trying to dig something out of the littlechange pocket in the front of her jeans. "Speaking of high."

She tossed two blue and white capsules onto the table. "What is that?" I asked.

"Oxycontin AR." She broke the first one in two. The white powder collected in a neat mound. "The doctors keep me pretty well stocked. Do you have a creditcard on you? I left mine back at the hotel."

Here she was, not all that long out of rehab, behaving the same as ever. I wasn't appalled. I wasn't even surprised. "I'll be right back." I headed inside to get my wallet. Trevor was sitting at the dining room table, talking on his cell phone. He glanced over and gave me a thumb-up. "Everything okay?" he mouthed.

What should I have said? Everything is going just fine. We've been discussing Rachael's newly discovered propensity to lick boots, Hector's downfall, and now we're about to wind things up with a few fat lines of Oxycontin. Instead, I gave him a wink and a nod.

I grabbed my credit card and a dollar bill and headed back out to the deck. Rachael had broken the other capsule open, creating a second heaping pile. I handed her the credit card.

"Thanks," she said, and began cutting the powder into lines. Watching her felt like putting on a pair of comfortable old slippers. For the first time in a long time, I didn't have to worry about what I was going to do or say next or how to explain the excesses of our relationship. So what if this wasn't me anymore. It was precisely who I used to be. And it was all Rachael and I ever were. The thing that doomed me and Rachael wasn't her drug use or my affair. It was the conversation we just hadn't had. We were role players, supporting actors in each other's stories, playing out some kind of mutual fantasy. Neither one of us had been willing to step into the leading role, or, better yet, set the script aside and improvise a real life. And now, it was too late. Even so, it was only at this moment that I felt any real connection to her. A mound of powder piled on a glass-topped table was as close as Rachael and I ever came, ever would come, to intimacy.

I gave Rachael the rolled-up bill, and she did her line. She handed the bill back to me.

"Want one?" she asked. "For old time's sake."

Rachael and I would end the way we had started. High. There was a certain elegant, twisted symmetry in that.

I took the bill from her, came up halfway from the chair and did the fattest one, top to bottom.

I felt it right away, like the finest sandpaper smoothing all the rough edges the Valium had missed. I sat back down and, for the first time, looked Rachael right in the eyes. Rachael smiled. Teary and sad. She slid her hand across the table toward me. I did the same and pressed it forward until the tips of my fingers touched hers.

"You know," she said, "I really should go."

I didn't want to break our fragile little connection. But what was there left to say?

Rachael stood. "I hope you find what you're looking for."

"If I do, I'll send it your way." I paused. "Deal?"

She smiled. "Deal."

37

South Pointe

I hooked my thumbs onto the chain link fence surrounding the perimeter of the Winter Party and leaned my weight against it. On either side of me, two-story banks of speakers lined the football-length dance area set on Twelfth Street, not fifty yards from the ocean. Inside, hundreds of people danced and milled around. It was a good day for a party: sunny, not too hot, with a steady breeze off the water. For a second, I got that pulse-quickening stab—I wanted in. I rocked back and forth to the music, scanning the crowd for a familiar face. I walked once around the perimeter, past hundreds of shirtless men. I had told myself I was taking a casual stroll. Who was I kidding? That was like feigning interest in all the new releases at the video store when you knew damn well you were there for the porn. I guess I had wanted to see how it would feel. Familiar? Foreign? Enticing? Abhorrent? Yeah, it was all those things.

A few months earlier, my endless summer in Provincetown had finally run up against fall. What next? Why not Miami? Why *not* Miami. I rented a pickup, strapped everything I owned to it, and took off. I had found a little studio near Flamingo Park in South Beach, not much bigger than the place I lived when I met Rachael, and settled in. Sure, it could fit into the master bedroom of our former house in D.C. with room to spare, but it was, after applying a decade's worth of decorating techniques I'd picked up from Rachael and the boys, cute, stylish—and mine.

I hadn't known what to expect from South Beach. Though the place looked the same, things had definitely changed. Gianni Versace had been shot dead standing right outside his mansion on Ocean Drive, the Warsaw Ballroom had become a deli, and club Salvation an office supply store. South Beach had become solidly, undeniably mainstream. The artist, models, and celebrities who had established the place had been replaced by tourists from Indiana snapping pictures of Ocean Drive from the top of the Duck Tour bus.

The Beach wasn't the only thing that had changed. So, seemingly, had what it meant to be gay. Funny thing, as I had become gayer in my sensibilities and lifestyle, gay society had become straighter. The heart of the gay scene—made up partly of men given new, unexpected futures courtesy the protease inhibitors which kept their HIV in check—had packed up and moved north to Ft. Lauderdale. There, they renovated houses in quiet neighborhoods, adopted kids, and live lives in most ways undistinguishable from their straight neighbors.

So, *they* had moved on. Had I? The years I'd spent with the boys had been a serendipitous courtship, "a beautiful friendship," as Bogey put it to Claude Rains at the end of *Casablanca*. I had hitched a ride on the rainbow-colored party float at exactly the right time, just as the ticker-tape parade turned, triumphant, down Fifth Avenue. In the end, of course, we had to part ways. The differences, as Trevor had pointed out, may have been irreconcilable, but the parting was amicable. And, like all relationships—even the failed ones—this one left its mark upon me. Yes, the queens had, by their acceptance and through their example, shown me how to be a man. I had no doubt that a part of me would remain, proudly, the gayest straight man in America.

My reentry into a single hetero lifestyle had not been all smooth sailing, though. My straight guy muscles had been severely atrophied. The few times I had gotten up the nerve to approach a woman, I'd encountered, at best, a wary indifference. The straight club scene was something of a mystery to me. Yes, it had copped many of the external trappings from the gay clubs—the music, the lights and the cult of the deejay—but there was a hard edge to it, driven by the coyness of the girls and the macho posturing of the men. It lacked that elusive buzz—the sense of unity, the white-hot energy that slammed you right up against the wall and kept you coming back for more. A few gay clubs remained, and a couple of the circuit parties continued to roll through, but Miami Beach's era as a gay mecca had passed, and with it the heart of the place, at least as far as I was concerned. Now, it all felt like one big frat party, visited by trashed college kids on spring break, goombahs, and hip-hop home boys trolling the beach, videotaping unsuspecting girls.

That's not to say that the place didn't have its moments. Walking along the beach, I would hear a low rumble and look up to see a cigarette boat, sleek and fast, skipping over the waves. Sure, Miami was changing, but that had always been part of its appeal. Recent waves of immigrants from South America, France, Italy, and Central Europe had given the place an international feel. "Come to Miami," the locals said, "it's *almost* like being in the USA." Steeped in the ubiquitous Latin rhythms I heard all around me, I bought a set of bongos. At sunset, I'd take them down to the beach and play. There was a buzz about the city, the energy of a boom town, the feeling that it was evolving, that was not yet what it would become. I had a feeling there was a future here for me. I just had to find my place in it.

The music slammed me with the sound of a party hitting its stride. I took a step back. Maybe I didn't know where I belonged, but if I had learned one thing, it was where I *didn't*.

I turned and walked along the beach, block after block, up against the water's edge, soft sand angling down gently to the shallow glimmer of the ocean. I didn't stop until I had to. The jetty at South Pointe was the very tip of South Beach—the end of the line. It was popular with the locals trying to keep their distance from the tourists and surfers chasing the waves caused by the jetty. A couple of hundred yards offshore, a dozen or so of them were fanned out in a sawtooth pattern, bobbing up and down in the swells. I climbed onto the hulking, jagged rocks that define the channel's northern flank. It was good place to watch the big cruise ships loom past as they headed from the harbor out to sea.

The music had lost its intensity, fading to a ragged buzz. I walked out along the jetty as far as I could go and only then allowed myself to turn back and look up the shore. I could just make out the multicolored floats and kites suspended in the sky above it. From this vantage point, the beach was as it appeared to me the first time had seen it—a lovely arc of pale gray and turquoise. I rubbed my eyes and took in a lungful of breeze. That kid working the door at the Crown said it: "The world—full of possibilities." Made me smile then and it still did.

I picked my way over the rocks, down to the sand and off the beach, away from the party, a head full of possibilities leading the way.

Epilogue

More than fifteen years have passed since the events depicted in this story. Those of us who didn't crash and burn moved on. Some of us did both.

Trevor's worst fears regarding Wes's business were realized. One Memorial Day weekend, the police raided the house. Wes would survive his stint in prison but his relationship with Trevor would not. They have moved on, but separately.

Dr. Hector continued his downward spiral. The man who had it all, lost it all: his medical license, his career, and very nearly his life. Following his three-year imprisonment for possession, he got, and, remains sober and active in the recovery community, working to organize clinical studies of medications that combat addiction. His is a story of descent and redemption that certainly deserves its own book. I hope he writes it.

My mother died of non-Hodgkin's lymphoma in 2009. Though she would not live to see me receive my MFA, finish this book, or meet my future wife, I feel her presence and her pride every day.

My father still lives in Washington, D.C., is happily married, and recently celebrated his thirty-nineth year of sobriety. He is my biggest fan. I am his.

David, who was set up by Rachael with one of her exceedingly rare straight, female friends (a former work colleague), was, and is, happily married and happily retired.

Trudie and I gave it a shot. We shouldn't have, but we did. It was much too soon, for both of us. We lasted a year. Trudie went on to establish a consulting firm that helps visual artists navigate their careers. I bet she's really good at it.

Rachael and I have had barely any contact since that afternoon on the deck of Trevor and Wes's house in Provincetown. Soon after our divorce, she sold the house and the business in D.C. and moved to another city in another state. I hope she found what she was looking for.

I did, but it sure didn't happen where, or when, or how I expected. Determined to write this memoir (obsessed is more like it) I sought out the advice and support of the Miami-based writing community, which is considerably larger, more cohesive, and more talented than it is given credit for. Eventually, I would overcome my resistance to returning to school at the age of fifty and entered a graduate program in creative writing, from which I graduated in 2011. That same year, I was invited to read an essay, adapted from this memoir, at a popular Miami-based live storytelling event. The essay begins with a scene in a hot tub on Fire Island. Yeah, *that* scene. Single at the time, I told the producer of the show that my story would be sure to send any and all eligible women in the audience running for the exits. In fact, I said, my essay would guarantee that I remained single for the rest of my life. Seated in the front row that night was a divorced physician with two children. Denise and I met at the show's after party. We were married a year later.

Fortunate doesn't begin to describe the turn of events that have led me to my new life as a stepfather to two smart and energetic teenaged boys and the husband of a beautiful and brilliant woman. These days, I live in the suburbs, drive a pickup truck, and yes, occasionally shop at Costco. I teach and work in the creative writing program at my alma matter, where I advise current and prospective students about the joys and horrors of writing. It's a very good life, better than I deserve. The story of my past became the pathway to my future. For that, I am indeed grateful.